MznLnx

Missing Links Exam Preps

Exam Prep for

Single Variable Calculus: Early Transcendentals

Stewart, 6th Edition

The MznLnx Exam Prep is your link from the texbook and lecture to your exams.
The MznLnx Exam Preps are unauthorized and comprehensive reviews of your textbooks.

All material provided by MznLnx and Rico Publications (c) 2010
Textbook publishers and textbook authors do not particpate in or contribute to these reviews.

MznLnx

Rico
Publications

Exam Prep for Single Variable Calculus: Early Transcendentals
6th Edition
Stewart

Publisher: Raymond Houge
Assistant Editor: Michael Rouger
Text and Cover Designer: Lisa Buckner
Marketing Manager: Sara Swagger
Project Manager, Editorial Production: Jerry Emerson
Art Director: Vernon Lowerui

Product Manager: Dave Mason
Editorial Assitant: Rachel Guzmanji
Pedagogy: Debra Long
Cover Image: Jim Reed/Getty Images
Text and Cover Printer: City Printing, Inc.
Compositor: Media Mix, Inc.

(c) 2010 Rico Publications
ALL RIGHTS RESERVED. No part of this work covered by the copyright may be reproduced or used in any form or by an means--graphic, electronic, or mechanical, including photocopying, recording, taping, Web distribution, information storage, and retrieval systems, or in any other manner--without the written permission of the publisher.

Printed in the United States
ISBN:

For more information about our products, contact us at:
Dave.Mason@RicoPublications.com

For permission to use material from this text or product, submit a request online to:
Dave.Mason@RicoPublications.com

Contents

CHAPTER 1
FUNCTIONS AND MODELS — 1

CHAPTER 2
LIMITS AND DERIVATIVES — 21

CHAPTER 3
DIFFERENTIATION RULES — 34

CHAPTER 4
APPLICATIONS OF DIFFERENTIATION — 58

CHAPTER 5
INTEGRALS — 72

CHAPTER 6
APPLICATIONS OF INTEGRATION — 78

CHAPTER 7
TECHNIQUES OF INTEGRATION — 88

CHAPTER 8
FURTHER APPLICATIONS OF INTEGRATION — 98

CHAPTER 9
DIFFERENTIAL EQUATIONS — 110

CHAPTER 10
PARAMETRIC EQUATIONS AND POLAR COORDINATES — 122

CHAPTER 11
INFINITE SEQUENCES AND SERIES — 138

ANSWER KEY — 160

TO THE STUDENT

COMPREHENSIVE

The *MznLnx* Exam Prep series is designed to help you pass your exams. Editors at MznLnx review your textbooks and then prepare these practice exams to help you master the textbook material. Unlike study guides, workbooks, and practice tests provided by the texbook publisher and textbook authors, *MznLnx* gives you **all** of the material in each chapter in exam form, not just samples, so you can be sure to nail your exam.

MECHANICAL

The MznLnx Exam Prep series creates exams that will help you learn the subject matter as well as test you on your understanding. Each question is designed to help you master the concept. Just working through the exams, you gain an understanding of the subject--its a simple mechanical process that produces success.

INTEGRATED STUDY GUIDE AND REVIEW

MznLnx is not just a set of exams designed to test you, its also a comprehensive review of the subject content. Each exam question is also a review of the concept, making sure that you will get the answer correct without having to go to other sources of material. You learn as you go! Its the easiest way to pass an exam.

HUMOR

Studying can be tedious and dry. MznLnx's instructional design includes moderate humor within the exam questions on occassion, to break the tedium and revitalize the brain

Chapter 1. FUNCTIONS AND MODELS

1. In mathematics, the concept of a '_____' is used to describe the behavior of a function as its argument or input either 'gets close' to some point, or as the argument becomes arbitrarily large; or the behavior of a sequence's elements as their index increases indefinitely. Limits are used in calculus and other branches of mathematical analysis to define derivatives and continuity.

In formulas, _____ is usually abbreviated as lim

   a. Limit
   b. BIBO stability
   c. 15 theorem
   d. BDDC

2. In probability theory and statistics, the _____ (or expectation value or mean and for continuous random variables with a density function it is the probability density -weighted integral of the possible values.

The term '_____' can be misleading.

   a. AUSM
   b. ALGOR
   c. ACTRAN
   d. Expected value

3. In calculus, the _____ states, roughly, that given a section of a smooth curve, there is at least one point on that section at which the derivative (slope) of the curve is equal (parallel) to the 'average' derivative of the section. It is used to prove theorems that make global conclusions about a function on an interval starting from local hypotheses about derivatives at points of the interval.

This theorem can be understood concretely by applying it to motion: If a car travels one hundred miles in one hour, so its average speed during that time was 100 miles per hour.

   a. First derivative test
   b. Mean Value Theorem
   c. Leibniz differential
   d. Fresnel integrals

4. The _____ is a method of finding the area of a shape by inscribing inside it a sequence of polygons whose areas converge to the area of the containing shape. If the sequence is correctly constructed, the difference in area between the nth polygon and the containing shape will become arbitrarily small as n becomes large. As this difference becomes arbitrarily small, the possible values for the area of the shape are systematically 'exhausted' by the lower bound areas successively established by the sequence members.

   a. Method of exhaustion
   b. BIBO stability
   c. 15 theorem
   d. BDDC

5. In mathematics, a _____ is an ordered list of objects (or events). Like a set, it contains members (also called elements or terms), and the number of terms (possibly infinite) is called the length of the _____. Unlike a set, order matters, and the exact same elements can appear multiple times at different positions in the _____.

   a. Sequence
   b. BDDC
   c. Y-intercept
   d. 15 theorem

6. In mathematics, the _____ is a criterion for the convergence (a convergence test) of an infinite series

$$\sum_{n=1}^{\infty} a_n.$$

It is particularly useful in connection with power series.

The _____ was developed first by Cauchy and so is sometimes known as the Cauchy _____ or Cauchy's radical test. The _____ uses the number

$$C = \limsup_{n \to \infty} \sqrt[n]{|a_n|},$$

where 'lim sup' denotes the limit superior, possibly ∞.

   a. Binomial series   b. Related rates
   c. Dirichlet integral   d. Root Test

7. The _____, named after the mathematician Ehrenfried Walther von Tschirnhaus, is a plane curve which is defined by either of these formulae:

$y^2 = x^3 + 3x^2$

$a = r\cos^3(\theta / 3.)$

   a. Strophoid   b. Dolbeault operator
   c. Tschirnhausen cubic   d. Kampyle of Eudoxus

8. In mathematics, a (topological) _____ is defined as follows: let I be an interval of real numbers (i.e. a non-empty connected subset of $\mathbb{R}$); then a _____ γ is a continuous mapping $\gamma : I \to X$, where X is a topological space. The _____ γ is said to be simple if it is injective, i.e. if for all x, y in I, we have $\gamma(x) = \gamma(y) \implies x = y$. If I is a closed bounded interval $[a, b]$, we also allow the possibility $\gamma(a) = \gamma(b)$ (this convention makes it possible to talk about closed simple _____.)

   a. Tractrix   b. Curve
   c. Closed curve   d. Prolate cycloid

9. In geometry, the _____ (or simply the tangent) to a curve at a given point is the straight line that 'just touches' the curve at that point (in the sense explained more precisely below.) As it passes through the point of tangency, the _____ is 'going in the same direction' as the curve, and in this sense it is the best straight-line approximation to the curve at that point. The same definition applies to space curves and curves in n-dimensional Euclidean space.

   a. Lie derivative   b. Sphere
   c. Minimal surface   d. Tangent line

10. In physics, _____ is defined as the rate of change of position. it is vector physical quantity; both speed and direction are required to define it. In the SI (metric) system, it is measured in meters per second: (m/s) or ms^{-1}.

a. BDDC
b. BIBO stability
c. 15 theorem
d. Velocity

11. In calculus, a branch of mathematics, the _____ is a measurement of how a function changes when its input changes. Loosely speaking, a _____ can be thought of as how much a quantity is changing at some given point. For example, the _____ of the position (or distance) of a vehicle with respect to time is the instantaneous velocity (respectively, instantaneous speed) at which the vehicle is traveling.

The process of finding a _____ is called differentiation. The fundamental theorem of calculus states that differentiation is the reverse process to integration.

a. Concave upwards
b. Ramp function
c. Mountain pass theorem
d. Derivative

12. Let f be a differentiable function, and let f'(x) be its derivative. The derivative of f'(x) (if it has one) is written f''(x) and is called the _____ of f. Similarly, the derivative of a _____, if it exists, is written f'''(x) and is called the third derivative of f.

a. Stationary phase approximation
b. Ramp function
c. Horizontal asymptote
d. Second Derivative

13. In calculus, a branch of mathematics, the _____ is a criterion often useful for determining whether a given stationary point of a function is a local maximum or a local minimum.

The test states: If the function f is twice differentiable at a stationary point x, meaning that $f'(x) = 0$, then:

- If $f''(x) < 0$ then f has a local maximum at x.
- If $f''(x) > 0$ then f has a local minimum at x.
- If $f''(x) = 0$, the _____ says nothing about the point x, has a possible inflection point.

In the last case, the function may have a local maximum or minimum there, but the function is sufficiently 'flat' that this is undetected by the second derivative. In this case one has to examine the third derivative. Such an example is f(x) = x⁴.

a. Parametric derivative
b. Stationary point
c. Metric derivative
d. Second Derivative Test

14. _____ are a set of problems generally thought to have been devised by Zeno of Elea to support Parmenides's doctrine that 'all is one' and that, contrary to the evidence of our senses, the belief in plurality and change is mistaken, and in particular that motion is nothing but an illusion. It is usually assumed, based on Plato's Parmenides 128c-d, that Zeno took on the project of creating these paradoxes because other philosophers had created paradoxes against Parmenides's view. Thus Zeno can be interpreted as saying that to assume there is plurality is even more absurd than assuming there is only 'the One' (Parmenides 128d.)

Chapter 1. FUNCTIONS AND MODELS

a. BIBO stability
c. Zeno's paradoxes

b. 15 theorem
d. BDDC

15. In calculus, the _____ is a method of finding the derivative of a function that is the quotient of two other functions for which derivatives exist.

If the function one wishes to differentiate, f(x), can be written as

$$f(x) = \frac{g(x)}{h(x)}$$

and h(x) ≠ 0, then the rule states that the derivative of g(x) / h(x) is equal to:

$$\frac{d}{dx}f(x) = f'(x) = \frac{g'(x)h(x) - g(x)h'(x)}{[h(x)]^2}.$$

Or, more precisely, if all x in some open set containing the number a satisfy h(x) ≠ 0; and g'(a) and h'(a) both exist; then, f'(a) exists as well and:

$$f'(a) = \frac{g'(a)h(a) - g(a)h'(a)}{[h(a)]^2}.$$

The derivative of (4x − 2) / (x² + 1) is:

$$\frac{d}{dx}\left[\frac{(4x-2)}{x^2+1}\right] = \frac{(x^2+1)(4) - (4x-2)(2x)}{(x^2+1)^2}$$

$$= \frac{(4x^2+4) - (8x^2-4x)}{(x^2+1)^2} = \frac{-4x^2+4x+4}{(x^2+1)^2}$$

In the example above, the choices

g(x) = 4x − 2
h(x) = x² + 1

were made. Analogously, the derivative of sin(x) / x² (when x ≠ 0) is:

$$\frac{\cos(x)x^2 - \sin(x)2x}{x^4}$$

Another example is:

$$f(x) = \frac{2x^2}{x^3}$$

whereas g(x) = 2x² and h(x) = x³, and g'(x) = 4x and h'(x) = 3x².

a. Product rule
b. Reciprocal Rule
c. Quotient Rule
d. Differentiation rules

16. In calculus, the _____ is a shorthand method of finding the derivative of a function that is the reciprocal of a differentiable function, without using the quotient rule or chain rule.

The _____ states that the derivative of 1 / g(x) is given by

$$\frac{d}{dx}\left(\frac{1}{g(x)}\right) = \frac{-g'(x)}{(g(x))^2}$$

where $g(x) \neq 0$.

The _____ is derived from the quotient rule, with the numerator f(x) = 1. Then,

It is also possible to derive the _____ from the chain rule, by a process very much like that of the derivation of the quotient rule.

a. Quotient Rule
b. Differentiation rules
c. Constant factor rule in differentiation
d. Reciprocal Rule

17. The terms '_____' and 'independent variable' are used in similar but subtly different ways in mathematics and statistics as part of the standard terminology in those subjects. They are used to distinguish between two types of quantities being considered, separating them into those available at the start of a process and those being created by it, where the latter (dependent variables) are dependent on the former (independent variables.)

In traditional calculus, a function is defined as a relation between two terms called variables because their values vary.

a. BIBO stability
b. 15 theorem
c. BDDC
d. Dependent variable

18. In mathematics, the _____ (or replacement set) of a given function is the set of 'input' values for which the function is defined. For instance, the _____ of cosine would be all real numbers, while the _____ of the square root would be only numbers greater than or equal to 0 (ignoring complex numbers in both cases.) In a representation of a function in a xy Cartesian coordinate system, the _____ is represented on the x axis (or abscissa.)
   a. BDDC
   b. 15 theorem
   c. BIBO stability
   d. Domain

19. The terms 'dependent variable' and '_____' are used in similar but subtly different ways in mathematics and statistics as part of the standard terminology in those subjects. They are used to distinguish between two types of quantities being considered, separating them into those available at the start of a process and those being created by it, where the latter (dependent variables) are dependent on the former (independent variables.)

In traditional calculus, a function is defined as a relation between two terms called variables because their values vary.

   a. ACTRAN
   b. AUSM
   c. ALGOR
   d. Independent variable

20. In mathematics, the _____ of a function is the set of all 'output' values produced by that function. Sometimes it is called the image, or more precisely, the image of the domain of the function. If a function is a surjection then its _____ is equal to its codomain.
   a. Constant function
   b. Piecewise-defined function
   c. Surjective
   d. Range

21. A _____ or Gompertz function, named after Benjamin Gompertz, is a sigmoid function. It is a type of mathematical model for a time series, where growth is slowest at the start and end of a time period. Graphs of Gompertz curves, showing the effect of varying one of a,b,c while keeping the others constant.

$$y(t) = ae^{be^{ct}}$$

where

- a is the upper asymptote
- c is the growth rate
- b, c are negative numbers
- e is Euler's Number (e = 2.71828...)

The function curve can be derived from Gompertz's law, which states the rate of mortality (decay) falls exponentially with current size. Mathematically

$$k^r \propto \frac{1}{y(t)}$$

where

- $r = \dfrac{y'(t)}{y(t)}$ is the rate of growth.
- k is an arbitrary constant.

Examples of uses for Gompertz curves include:

- Mobile phone uptake, where costs were initially high (so uptake was slow), followed by a period of rapid growth, followed by a slowing of uptake as saturation was reached.
- Population in a confined space, as birth rates first increase and then slow as resource limits are reached.
- Modeling of growth of tumors

In the sixties A.K. Laird for the first time successfully used the _____ to fit data of growth of tumors. In fact, tumors are cellular populations growing in a confined space where the availability of nutrients is limited.

a. Spheroidal wave functions
b. Duffing equation
c. Neumann-Dirichlet method
d. Gompertz curve

22. The _____ are a pair of first order, non-linear, differential equations frequently used to describe the dynamics of biological systems in which two species interact, one a predator and one its prey. They were proposed independently by Alfred J. Lotka in 1925 and Vito Volterra in 1926.

>

>

where

- y is the number of some predator;
- x is the number of its prey;
- dy/dt and dx/dt represents the growth of the two populations against time;
- t represents the time; and
- >α, >β, >γ and >δ are parameters representing the interaction of the two species.

When multiplied out, the equations take a form useful for physical interpretation. Their origin should be considered from a more general framework,

where both functions represent per capita growth rates of the prey and predator, respectively.

   a. 15 theorem
   b. Lotka-Volterra equations
   c. BIBO stability
   d. BDDC

23. In mathematics, the _____ is a representation of a function as an infinite sum of terms calculated from the values of its derivatives at a single point. It may be regarded as the limit of the Taylor polynomials. If the series is centered at zero, the series is also called a Maclaurin series.

   a. BDDC
   b. 15 theorem
   c. BIBO stability
   d. Taylor series

24. A _____ is a type of display using Cartesian coordinates to display values for two variables for a set of data. The data is displayed as a collection of points, each having the value of one variable determining the position on the horizontal axis and the value of the other variable determining the position on the vertical axis.

   a. BDDC
   b. BIBO stability
   c. 15 theorem
   d. Scatter plot

25. The _____ is a test to determine if a relation or its graph is a function or not. For a relation or graph to be a function, it can have at most a single y-value for each x-value. Thus, a vertical line drawn at any x-position on the graph of a function will intersect the graph at most once.

   a. 15 theorem
   b. BIBO stability
   c. BDDC
   d. Vertical Line Test

26. In mathematics, the _____ (or modulus) of a real number is its numerical value without regard to its sign. So, for example, 3 is the _____ of both 3 and −3.

The _____ of a number a is denoted by $|a|$.

   a. Area hyperbolic functions
   b. Exponential function
   c. ACTRAN
   d. Absolute value

27. In mathematics, a _____ is a function whose definition is dependent on the value of the independent variable. Mathematically, a real-valued function f of a real variable x is a relationship whose definition is given differently on disjoint subsets of its domain

The word piecewise is also used to describe any property of a _____ that holds for each piece but may not hold for the whole domain of the function.

Chapter 1. FUNCTIONS AND MODELS

a. Constant function
b. Surjective
c. Piecewise-defined function
d. Range

28. In calculus, the _____ is a theorem regarding the limit of a function.

The _____ is a technical result which is very important in proofs in calculus and mathematical analysis. It is typically used to confirm the limit of a function via comparison with two other functions whose limits are known or easily computed.

a. Limit of a sequence
b. 15 theorem
c. Table of limits
d. Squeeze Theorem

29. A _____ is an algebraic equation in which each term is either a constant or the product of a constant and (the first power of) a single variable. Linear equations can have one, two, three or more variables. Linear equations occur with great regularity in applied mathematics.
a. Linear equation
b. Cubic function
c. BDDC
d. 15 theorem

30. In mathematics, a function on the real numbers is called a _____ (or staircase function) if it can be written as a finite linear combination of indicator functions of intervals. Informally speaking, a _____ is a piecewise constant function having only finitely many pieces.
a. Step function
b. Hyperbolic sine
c. Multiplicative inverse
d. Hyperbolic tangent

31. In mathematics, even functions and odd functions are functions which satisfy particular symmetry relations, with respect to taking additive inverses. They are important in many areas of mathematical analysis, especially the theory of power series and Fourier series. They are named for the parity of the powers of the power functions which satisfy each condition: the function $f(x) = x^n$ is an _____ if n is an even integer, and it is an odd function if n is an odd integer.
a. Infinite series
b. Operational calculus
c. Integral of secant cubed
d. Even function

32. In mathematics, even functions and odd functions are functions which satisfy particular symmetry relations, with respect to taking additive inverses. They are important in many areas of mathematical analysis, especially the theory of power series and Fourier series. They are named for the parity of the powers of the power functions which satisfy each condition: the function $f(x) = x^n$ is an even function if n is an even integer, and it is an _____ if n is an odd integer.
a. Integration by substitution
b. Integral of secant cubed
c. Even function
d. Odd function

33. _____ generally conveys two primary meanings. The first is an imprecise sense of harmonious or aesthetically-pleasing proportionality and balance; such that it reflects beauty or perfection. The second meaning is a precise and well-defined concept of balance or 'patterned self-similarity' that can be demonstrated or proved according to the rules of a formal system: by geometry, through physics or otherwise.
a. BIBO stability
b. 15 theorem
c. Symmetry
d. BDDC

Chapter 1. FUNCTIONS AND MODELS

34. In mathematics, a _____ is a function which preserves the given order. This concept first arose in calculus, and was later generalized to the more abstract setting of order theory.

In calculus, a function f defined on a subset of the real numbers with real values is called monotonic (also monotonically increasing or non-decreasing), if for all x and y such that x >≤ y one has f(x) >≤ f(y), so f preserves the order.

a. Pettis integral
b. Monotonic function
c. 15 theorem
d. Pseudo-differential operator

35. In statistics, given a (random) sample $(Y_i, X_{i1}, \ldots, X_{ip})$, $i = 1, \ldots, n$ the most general form of _____ is formulated as

$$Y_i = \beta_0 + \beta_1 \phi_1(X_{i1}) + \ldots + \beta_p \phi_p(X_{ip}) + \varepsilon_i \qquad i = 1, \ldots, n$$

where $\phi_1, \ldots, \phi_p$ may be nonlinear functions.

In matrix notation this model can be written as

$$Y = X\beta + \varepsilon$$

where Y is an n × 1 column vector, X is an n × (p + 1) matrix, β is a (p + 1) × 1 vector of (unobservable) parameters, and ε is an n × 1 vector of errors, which are uncorrelated random variables each with expected value 0 and variance σ^2. Note that depending on the context the sample can be seen as fixed (observable), or random.

a. BDDC
b. BIBO stability
c. 15 theorem
d. Linear model

36. In the mathematical field of numerical analysis, a _____ is a parametric curve important in computer graphics and related fields. Generalizations of Bezier curves to higher dimensions are called Bezier surfaces, of which the Bezier triangle is a special case.

Bezier curves were widely publicized in 1962 by the French engineer Pierre B>ézier, who used them to design automobile bodies.

a. BDDC
b. BIBO stability
c. 15 theorem
d. Bezier curve

37. _____ is finding a curve which has the best fit to a series of data points and possibly other constraints. This section is an introduction to both interpolation (where an exact fit to constraints is expected) and regression analysis. Both are sometimes used for extrapolation.

a. Series acceleration
b. Well-posed problem
c. Propagation of uncertainty
d. Curve fitting

Chapter 1. FUNCTIONS AND MODELS

38. In mathematical analysis, the _____ states that for each value between the least upper bound and greatest lower bound of the image of a continuous function there is a corresponding value in its domain mapping to the original. _____

- Version I. The _____ states the following: If the function y = f(x) is continuous on the interval [a, b], and u is a number between f(a) and f(b), then there is a c ∈ [a, b] such that f(c) = u.

- Version II. Suppose that I is an interval [a, b] in the real numbers R and that f : I → R is a continuous function. Then the image set f(I) is also an interval, and either it contains [f(a), f(b)], or it contains [f(b), f(a)]; that is,

    f(I) ⊇ [f(a), f(b)], or f(I) ⊇ [f(b), f(a)].

It is frequently stated in the following equivalent form: Suppose that f : [a, b] → R is continuous and that u is a real number satisfying f(a) < u < f(b) or f(a) > u > f(b).) Then for some c ∈ [a, b], f(c) = u.

This captures an intuitive property of continuous functions: given f continuous on [1, 2], if f(1) = 3 and f(2) = 5 then f must take the value 4 somewhere between 1 and 2.

    a. ALGOR
    c. Intermediate Value Theorem
    b. ACTRAN
    d. AUSM

39. In mathematics, _____ is the process of constructing new data points outside a discrete set of known data points. It is similar to the process of interpolation, which constructs new points between known points, but the results of extrapolations are often less meaningful, and are subject to greater uncertainty. Example illustration of the _____ problem, consisting of assigning a meaningful value at the blue box, at x = 7, given the red data points.

A sound choice of which _____ method to apply relies on a prior knowledge of the process that created the existing data points.

    a. ACTRAN
    c. AUSM
    b. ALGOR
    d. Extrapolation

40. In the mathematical subfield of numerical analysis, _____ is a method of constructing new data points within the range of a discrete set of known data points.

In engineering and science one often has a number of data points, as obtained by sampling or experimentation, and tries to construct a function which closely fits those data points. This is called curve fitting or regression analysis.

    a. ACTRAN
    c. ALGOR
    b. Interpolation
    d. AUSM

41. The method of _____ or ordinary _____ is used to solve overdetermined systems. _____ is often applied in statistical contexts, particularly regression analysis.

_____ can be interpreted as a method of fitting data. The best fit in the _____ sense is that instance of the model for which the sum of squared residuals has its least value, a residual being the difference between an observed value and the value given by the model.

- a. BDDC
- b. 15 theorem
- c. BIBO stability
- d. Least squares

42. In statistics, _____ is a form of regression analysis in which the relationship between one or more independent variables and another variable, called dependent variable, is modeled by a least squares function, called _____ equation. This function is a linear combination of one or more model parameters, called regression coefficients. A _____ equation with one independent variable represents a straight line.
    - a. Normal distribution
    - b. Poisson distribution
    - c. Standard deviation
    - d. Linear regression

43. In calculus, the _____ is a formula used to find the derivatives of products of functions. It may be stated thus:

$$(f \cdot g)' = f' \cdot g + f \cdot g'$$

or in the Leibniz notation thus:

$$\frac{d}{dx}(u \cdot v) = u \cdot \frac{dv}{dx} + v \cdot \frac{du}{dx}.$$

Discovery of this rule is credited to Gottfried Leibniz, who demonstrated it using differentials. Here is Leibniz's argument: Let u and v be two differentiable functions of x.

- a. Product Rule
- b. Quotient Rule
- c. Constant factor rule in differentiation
- d. Reciprocal Rule

44. In mathematics, a _____ is a function of the form

$$f(x) = ax^3 + bx^2 + cx + d,$$

where a is nonzero; or in other words, a polynomial of degree three. The derivative of a _____ is a quadratic function. The integral of a _____ is a quartic function.

- a. BDDC
- b. Linear equation
- c. 15 theorem
- d. Cubic function

45. When a polynomial is expressed as a sum or difference of terms (e.g., in standard or canonical form), the exponent of the term with the highest exponent is the _____. The degree of a term is the sum of the powers of each variable in the term. The words degree and order are used interchangeably.

Chapter 1. FUNCTIONS AND MODELS

a. Degree of the polynomial
c. Quadratic function

b. Coefficient
d. Sheffer sequence

46. A _____, in mathematics, is a polynomial function of the form $f(x) = ax^2 + bx + c$, where $a \neq 0$. The graph of a _____ is a parabola whose major axis is parallel to the y-axis.

The expression ax² + bx + c in the definition of a _____ is a polynomial of degree 2 or a 2nd degree polynomial, because the highest exponent of x is 2.

a. Degree of the polynomial
c. Constant term

b. Quadratic function
d. Coefficient

47. In mathematics, an _____ is informally a function which satisfies a polynomial equation whose coefficients are themselves polynomials. For example, an _____ in one variable x is a solution y for an equation

$$a_n(x)y^n + a_{n-1}(x)y^{n-1} + \cdots + a_0(x) = 0$$

where the coefficients $a_i(x)$ are polynomial functions of x. A function which is not algebraic is called a transcendental function.

a. ACTRAN
c. AUSM

b. ALGOR
d. Algebraic function

48. In mathematics, a _____ is any function which can be written as the ratio of two polynomial functions.

$$y = \frac{x^2 - 3x - 2}{x^2 - 4}$$

In the case of one variable, x, a _____ is a function of the form

$$f(x) = \frac{P(x)}{Q(x)}$$

where P and Q are polynomial function in x and Q is not the zero polynomial. The domain of f is the set of all points x for which the denominator Q(x) is not zero.

a. BDDC
c. 15 theorem

b. BIBO stability
d. Rational function

49. In mathematics, a _____ or reciprocal for a number x, denoted by $1/x$ or x^{-1}, is a number which when multiplied by x yields the multiplicative identity, 1. The _____ of x is also called the reciprocal of x. The _____ of a fraction p/q is q/p.

a. Multiplicative inverse
b. Square root function
c. Heaviside step function
d. Hyperbolic sine

50. In mathematics, the _____ is a way to approximately calculate the definite integral

$$\int_a^b f(x)\,dx.$$

The _____ works by approximating the region under the graph of the function f by a trapezoid and calculating its area. It follows that

$$\int_a^b f(x)\,dx \approx (b-a)\frac{f(a)+f(b)}{2}.$$

To calculate this integral more accurately, one first splits the interval of integration [a,b] into n smaller subintervals, and then applies the _____ on each of them. One obtains the composite _____:

$$\int_a^b f(x)\,dx \approx \frac{b-a}{n}\left[\frac{f(a)+f(b)}{2} + \sum_{k=1}^{n-1} f\left(a+k\frac{b-a}{n}\right)\right].$$

This can alternatively be written as:

$$\int_a^b f(x)\,dx \approx \frac{b-a}{2n}\left(f(x_0) + 2f(x_1) + 2f(x_2) + \cdots + 2f(x_{n-1}) + f(x_n)\right)$$

where

$$x_k = a + k\frac{b-a}{n},\ \text{for } k = 0, 1, \ldots, n$$

(one can also use a non-uniform grid.)

a. BIBO stability
b. BDDC
c. 15 theorem
d. Trapezoidal Rule

51. Trigonometry is a branch of mathematics that deals with triangles, particularly those plane triangles in which one angle has 90 degrees (right triangles.) Trigonometry deals with relationships between the sides and the angles of triangles and with the _____ functions, which describe those relationships.

Trigonometry has applications in both pure mathematics and in applied mathematics, where it is essential in many branches of science and technology.

Chapter 1. FUNCTIONS AND MODELS

    a. 15 theorem
    b. Trigonometric functions
    c. Trigonometric integrals
    d. Trigonometric

52. In mathematics, the _____ are functions of an angle. They are important in the study of triangles and modeling periodic phenomena, among many other applications. _____ are commonly defined as ratios of two sides of a right triangle containing the angle, and can equivalently be defined as the lengths of various line segments from a unit circle.
    a. Trigonometric integrals
    b. 15 theorem
    c. Trigonometric functions
    d. Trigonometric

53. The _____ is a function in mathematics. The application of this function to a value x is written as exp(x). Equivalently, this can be written in the form e^x, where e is a mathematical constant, the base of the natural logarithm, which equals approximately 2.718281828, and is also known as Euler's number.
    a. ACTRAN
    b. Area hyperbolic functions
    c. Exponential function
    d. Integral part

54. In mathematics, a _____ is the graph of the system of parametric equations

$$x = A \sin(at + \delta), \quad y = B \sin(bt),$$

which describes complex harmonic motion. This family of curves was investigated by Nathaniel Bowditch in 1815, and later in more detail by Jules Antoine Lissajous in 1857.

The appearance of the figure is highly sensitive to the ratio a/b.

    a. BIBO stability
    b. 15 theorem
    c. BDDC
    d. Lissajous curve

55. The function $\log_b(x)$ depends on both b and x, but the term _____ in standard usage refers to a function of the form $\log_b(x)$ in which the base b is fixed and so the only argument is x. Thus there is one _____ for each value of the base b (which must be positive and must differ from 1.) Viewed in this way, the base-b _____ is the inverse function of the exponential function b^x.
    a. Logarithm function
    b. 15 theorem
    c. BIBO stability
    d. BDDC

56. A _____ is a function that does not satisfy a polynomial equation whose coefficients are themselves polynomials, in contrast to an algebraic function, which does satisfy such an equation. In other words a _____ is a function which 'transcends' algebra in the sense that it cannot be expressed in terms of a finite sequence of the algebraic operations of addition, multiplication, and root extraction.

Examples of transcendental functions include the exponential function, the logarithm, and the trigonometric functions.

    a. BDDC
    b. BIBO stability
    c. 15 theorem
    d. Transcendental function

57. The _____, H, also called the unit step function, is a discontinuous function whose value is zero for negative argument and one for positive argument. It seldom matters what value is used for H, since H is mostly used as a distribution. The function is used in the mathematics of control theory and signal processing to represent a signal that switches on at a specified time and stays switched on indefinitely.
- a. Hyperbolic cosine
- b. Heaviside step function
- c. Signum function
- d. Hyperbolic functions

58. The _____ is an elementary unary real function, easily computable as the mean of its independent variable and its absolute value.

This function is applied in engineering (e.g., in the theory of DSP.) The name _____ can be derived by the look of its graph.

- a. Differential calculus
- b. Bounded function
- c. Monodromy
- d. Ramp function

59. In mathematics and its applications, _____ refers to finding the linear approximation to a function at a given point. In the study of dynamical systems, _____ is a method for assessing the local stability of an equilibrium point of a system of nonlinear differential equations or discrete dynamical systems. This method is used in fields such as engineering, physics, economics, and ecology.
- a. Point of inflection
- b. Linearization
- c. Stationary point
- d. Symmetrically continuous

60. The largest and the smallest element of a set are called extreme values, absolute extrema, or extreme records.

For a differentiable function f, if $f(x_0)$ is an _____ for the set of all values f(x), and if x_0 is in the interior of the domain of f, then x_0 is a critical point, by Fermat's theorem.

In the case of a general partial order one should not confuse a least element (smaller than all other) and a minimal element (nothing is smaller.)

- a. Integration by substitution
- b. Infinitesimal
- c. Extreme Value Theorem
- d. Extreme Value

61. In calculus, the _____ states that if a real-valued function f is continuous in the closed and bounded interval [a,b], then f must attain its maximum and minimum value, each at least once. That is, there exist numbers c and d in [a,b] such that:

A related theorem is the boundedness theorem which states that a continuous function f in the closed interval [a,b] is bounded on that interval. That is, there exist real numbers m and M such that:

The _____ enriches the boundedness theorem by saying that not only is the function bounded, but it also attains its least upper bound as its maximum and its greatest lower bound as its minimum.

a. Infinitesimal
b. Uniform convergence
c. Extreme Value Theorem
d. Integral of secant cubed

62. In mathematics, a _____ is a unicursal quartic curve with three inflection points, given by the equation

$$a^2 y^2 - b^2 x^2 = x^2 y^2$$

The bullet curve has three double points in the real projective plane, at x=0 and y=0, x=0 and z=0, and y=0 and z=0, and is therefore a unicursal (rational) curve of genus zero.

If

$$f(z) = \sum_{n=0}^{\infty} \binom{2n}{n} z^{2n+1} = z + 2z^3 + 6z^5 + 20z^7 + \cdots$$

then

$$y = f\left(\frac{x}{2a}\right) \pm 2b$$

are the two branches of the bullet curve at the origin.

a. Bullet-nose curve
b. Folium of Descartes
c. Closed curve
d. Hypocycloid

63. In mathematics, the _____ of a function y = f(x) is a function that, in some fashion, 'undoes' the effect of f The _____ of f is denoted f^{-1}. The statements y=f(x) and x=f^{-1}(y) are equivalent.

a. AUSM
b. ALGOR
c. ACTRAN
d. Inverse

64. In mathematics, if f is a function from A to B then an _____ for f is a function in the opposite direction, from B to A, with the property that a round trip (a composition) from A to B to A (or from B to A to B) returns each element of the initial set to itself. Thus, if an input x into the function f produces an output y, then inputting y into the _____ f^{-1} (read f inverse, not to be confused with exponentiation) produces the output x. Not every function has an inverse; those that do are called invertible.

a. Inverse function
b. Augustin-Jean Fresnel
c. Aristotle
d. Augustin Louis Cauchy

65. In mathematics, the _____ is a test used to determine if a function is injective, surjective or bijective.

Suppose there is a function f : X → Y with a graph., and you have a horizontal line of X x Y :
$$y_0 \in Y, \{(x, y_0) : x \in X\} = (X \times y_0)$$

- If the function is injective, then it can be visualized as one whose graph is never intersected by any horizontal line more than once.
- If and only if f is surjective, any horizontal line will intersect the graph at least at one point (when the horizontal line is in the codomain.)
- If f is bijective, any horizontal line will intersect the graph at exactly one point.

This test is also used to find whether or not the inverse of the function is indeed a function as well. This is due to the reflective properties of the function over y=x.

a. BDDC
b. 15 theorem
c. BIBO stability
d. Horizontal Line Test

66. An injective function is called an injection, and is also said to be a _____ function (not to be confused with _____ correspondence, i.e. a bijective function.)

A function f that is not injective is sometimes called many-to-one. (However, this terminology is also sometimes used to mean 'single-valued', i.e. each argument is mapped to at most one value.)

a. Injective function
b. One-to-one
c. Onto
d. One-to-one function

67. An injective function is called an injection, and is also said to be a _____ (not to be confused with one-to-one correspondence, i.e. a bijective function.)

A function f that is not injective is sometimes called many-to-one. (However, this terminology is also sometimes used to mean 'single-valued', i.e. each argument is mapped to at most one value.)

a. Onto
b. Injective function
c. One-to-one
d. One-to-one function

68. In a totally ordered set all elements are mutually comparable, so such a set can have at most one minimal element and at most one maximal element. Then, due to mutual comparability, the minimal element will also be the least element and the maximal element will also be the greatest element. Thus in a totally ordered set we can simply use the terms minimum and _____.

a. Complex analysis
b. Dirichlet integral
c. Hyperbolic angle
d. Maximum

69. In calculus, the _____ is a formula for the derivative of the composite of two functions.

In intuitive terms, if a variable, y, depends on a second variable, u, which in turn depends on a third variable, x, then the rate of change of y with respect to x can be computed as the rate of change of y with respect to u multiplied by the rate of change of u with respect to x. Schematically,

$$\frac{dy}{dx} = \frac{dy}{du} \cdot \frac{du}{dx}.$$

a. Quotient Rule
b. Chain Rule
c. Differentiation rules
d. Reciprocal Rule

70. In mathematics, the _____ or cyclometric functions are the inverse functions of the trigonometric functions. The principal inverses are listed in the following table.

If x is allowed to be a complex number, then the range of y applies only to its real part.

a. AUSM
b. ALGOR
c. ACTRAN
d. Inverse trigonometric functions

71. This article will state and prove the _____ for differentiation, and then use it to prove these two formulas.

The _____ for differentiation states that for every natural number n, the derivative of $f(x) = x^n$ is $f'(x) = nx^{n-1}$, that is,

$$(x^n)' = nx^{n-1}.$$

The _____ for integration

$$\int x^n \, dx = \frac{x^{n+1}}{n+1} + C$$

for natural n is then an easy consequence. One just needs to take the derivative of this equality and use the _____ and linearity of differentiation on the right-hand side.

a. Dirichlet integral
b. Limits of integration
c. Hyperbolic angle
d. Power Rule

72. _____ is a method of mathematical proof typically used to establish that a given statement is true of all natural numbers. It is done by proving that the first statement in the infinite sequence of statements is true, and then proving that if any one statement in the infinite sequence of statements is true, then so is the next one.

The method can be extended to prove statements about more general well-founded structures, such as trees; this generalization, known as structural induction, is used in mathematical logic and computer science.

a. 15 theorem
b. Mathematical induction
c. BIBO stability
d. BDDC

Chapter 2. LIMITS AND DERIVATIVES

1. In calculus, the _____ determines whether a given critical point of a function is a maximum, a minimum, or neither.

Suppose that f is a function and we want to determine if f has a maximum or minimum at x. If f is increasing to the left of x and decreasing to the right of x, then x is a local maximum of f.

- a. Hyperbolic angle
- b. Functional integration
- c. Test for Divergence
- d. First Derivative Test

2. In mathematics, the concept of a '_____' is used to describe the behavior of a function as its argument or input either 'gets close' to some point, or as the argument becomes arbitrarily large; or the behavior of a sequence's elements as their index increases indefinitely. Limits are used in calculus and other branches of mathematical analysis to define derivatives and continuity.

In formulas, _____ is usually abbreviated as lim

- a. BIBO stability
- b. 15 theorem
- c. BDDC
- d. Limit

3. In mathematics, a _____ is an ordered list of objects (or events). Like a set, it contains members (also called elements or terms), and the number of terms (possibly infinite) is called the length of the _____. Unlike a set, order matters, and the exact same elements can appear multiple times at different positions in the _____.

- a. 15 theorem
- b. Y-intercept
- c. BDDC
- d. Sequence

4. In geometry, the _____ (or simply the tangent) to a curve at a given point is the straight line that 'just touches' the curve at that point (in the sense explained more precisely below.) As it passes through the point of tangency, the _____ is 'going in the same direction' as the curve, and in this sense it is the best straight-line approximation to the curve at that point. The same definition applies to space curves and curves in n-dimensional Euclidean space.

- a. Sphere
- b. Minimal surface
- c. Lie derivative
- d. Tangent line

5. The _____, named after the mathematician Ehrenfried Walther von Tschirnhaus, is a plane curve which is defined by either of these formulae:

$y^2 = x^3 + 3x^2$

$a = r\cos^3(\theta / 3.)$

- a. Strophoid
- b. Kampyle of Eudoxus
- c. Dolbeault operator
- d. Tschirnhausen cubic

6. In physics, _____ is defined as the rate of change of position. it is vector physical quantity; both speed and direction are required to define it. In the SI (metric) system, it is measured in meters per second: (m/s) or ms^{-1}.

a. BIBO stability
b. Velocity
c. 15 theorem
d. BDDC

7. In calculus, the _____ is a method of finding the derivative of a function that is the quotient of two other functions for which derivatives exist.

If the function one wishes to differentiate, f(x), can be written as

$$f(x) = \frac{g(x)}{h(x)}$$

and h(x) ≠ 0, then the rule states that the derivative of g(x) / h(x) is equal to:

$$\frac{d}{dx}f(x) = f'(x) = \frac{g'(x)h(x) - g(x)h'(x)}{[h(x)]^2}.$$

Or, more precisely, if all x in some open set containing the number a satisfy h(x) ≠ 0; and g'(a) and h'(a) both exist; then, f'(a) exists as well and:

$$f'(a) = \frac{g'(a)h(a) - g(a)h'(a)}{[h(a)]^2}.$$

The derivative of (4x − 2) / (x² + 1) is:

$$\frac{d}{dx}\left[\frac{(4x-2)}{x^2+1}\right] = \frac{(x^2+1)(4) - (4x-2)(2x)}{(x^2+1)^2}$$

$$= \frac{(4x^2+4) - (8x^2-4x)}{(x^2+1)^2} = \frac{-4x^2+4x+4}{(x^2+1)^2}$$

In the example above, the choices

g(x) = 4x − 2
h(x) = x² + 1

were made. Analogously, the derivative of sin(x) / x² (when x ≠ 0) is:

$$\frac{\cos(x)x^2 - \sin(x)2x}{x^4}$$

Another example is:

$$f(x) = \frac{2x^2}{x^3}$$

whereas g(x) = 2x² and h(x) = x³, and g'(x) = 4x and h'(x) = 3x².

- a. Quotient Rule
- b. Differentiation rules
- c. Reciprocal Rule
- d. Product rule

8. In mathematics, the _____ is a criterion for the convergence (a convergence test) of an infinite series

$$\sum_{n=1}^{\infty} a_n.$$

It is particularly useful in connection with power series.

The _____ was developed first by Cauchy and so is sometimes known as the Cauchy _____ or Cauchy's radical test.
The _____ uses the number

$$C = \limsup_{n \to \infty} \sqrt[n]{|a_n|},$$

where 'lim sup' denotes the limit superior, possibly ∞.

- a. Dirichlet integral
- b. Binomial series
- c. Root Test
- d. Related rates

9. The _____, H, also called the unit step function, is a discontinuous function whose value is zero for negative argument and one for positive argument. It seldom matters what value is used for H, since H is mostly used as a distribution. The function is used in the mathematics of control theory and signal processing to represent a signal that switches on at a specified time and stays switched on indefinitely.
- a. Hyperbolic cosine
- b. Signum function
- c. Hyperbolic functions
- d. Heaviside step function

10. In mathematics, a _____ is a method for approximating the total area underneath a curve on a graph, otherwise known as an integral. It may also be used to define the integration operation.

Consider a function $f: D \rightarrow \mathbf{R}$, where D is a subset of the real numbers $\mathbf{R}$, and let $I = [a, b]$ be a closed interval contained in D. A finite set of points $\{x_0, x_1, x_2, \ldots x_n\}$ such that $a = x_0 < x_1 < x_2 \ldots < x_n = b$ creates a partition

$$P = \{[x_0, x_1), [x_1, x_2), \ldots [x_{n-1}, x_n]\}$$

of I.

    a. Disk integration   b. Riemann sum
    c. Signed measure   d. Surface of revolution

11. The _____ is a function in mathematics. The application of this function to a value x is written as exp(x). Equivalently, this can be written in the form e^x, where e is a mathematical constant, the base of the natural logarithm, which equals approximately 2.718281828, and is also known as Euler's number.
    a. Exponential function   b. Integral part
    c. ACTRAN   d. Area hyperbolic functions

12. In calculus, a _____ is either of the two limits of a function f(x) of a real variable x as x approaches a specified point either from below or from above. One should write either:

$$\lim_{x \to a^+} f(x) \text{ or } \lim_{x \downarrow a} f(x)$$

for the limit as x decreases in value approaching a (x approaches a 'from above' or 'from the right'), and similarly

$$\lim_{x \to a^-} f(x) \text{ or } \lim_{x \uparrow a} f(x)$$

for the limit as x increases in value approaching a (x approaches a 'from below' or 'from the left'.)

The two one-sided limits exist and are equal if and only if the limit of f(x) as x approaches a exists.

    a. ACTRAN   b. One-sided Limit
    c. AUSM   d. ALGOR

13. Cantor defined two kinds of _____ numbers, the ordinal numbers and the cardinal numbers. Ordinal numbers may be identified with well-ordered sets, or counting carried on to any stopping point, including points after an _____ number have already been counted. Generalizing finite and the ordinary _____ sequences which are maps from the positive integers leads to mappings from ordinal numbers, and transfinite sequences.
    a. AUSM   b. Infinite
    c. ACTRAN   d. ALGOR

14. An _____ of a real-valued function y = f(x) is a curve which describes the behavior of f as either x or y tends to infinity.

In other words, as one moves along the graph of f(x) in some direction, the distance between it and the _____ eventually becomes smaller than any distance that one may specify.

a. ACTRAN
c. AUSM
b. Asymptote
d. ALGOR

15. The line x = a is a _____ of a curve y=f(x) if at least one of the following statements is true:

1. $\lim_{x \to a} f(x) = \pm\infty$
2. $\lim_{x \to a^-} f(x) = \pm\infty$
3. $\lim_{x \to a^+} f(x) = \pm\infty$

Intuitively, if x = a is an asymptote of f, then, if we imagine x approaching a from one side, the value of f(x) grows without bound; i.e., f(x) becomes large (positively or negatively), and, in fact, becomes larger than any finite value.

Note that f(x) may or may not be defined at a: what the function is doing precisely at x = a does not affect the asymptote. For example, consider the function

$$f(x) = \begin{cases} \frac{1}{x} & \text{if } x > 0, \\ 5 & \text{if } x \leq 0 \end{cases}$$

As $\lim_{x \to 0^+} f(x) = \infty$, f(x) has a _____ at 0, even though f(0) = 5.

Another example is $f(x) = 1/(x-1)$ which has a _____ of x=1 as shown by the limit

$$\lim_{x \to 1^+} \frac{1}{x-1} = \infty$$

In the graph of $f(x) = x + \frac{1}{x}$, the y-axis (x = 0) and the line y = x are both asymptotes.

When a linear asymptote is not parallel to the x- or y-axis, it is called either an oblique asymptote or equivalently a slant asymptote.

a. Semi-differentiability
c. Geometric function theory
b. Fractional calculus
d. Vertical asymptote

16. In mathematics, a _____ is the graph of the system of parametric equations

$$x = A\sin(at+\delta), \quad y = B\sin(bt),$$

which describes complex harmonic motion. This family of curves was investigated by Nathaniel Bowditch in 1815, and later in more detail by Jules Antoine Lissajous in 1857.

The appearance of the figure is highly sensitive to the ratio a/b.

 a. BDDC
 b. 15 theorem
 c. BIBO stability
 d. Lissajous curve

17. The function $\log_b(x)$ depends on both b and x, but the term _____ in standard usage refers to a function of the form $\log_b(x)$ in which the base b is fixed and so the only argument is x. Thus there is one _____ for each value of the base b (which must be positive and must differ from 1.) Viewed in this way, the base-b _____ is the inverse function of the exponential function b^x.

 a. Logarithm function
 b. 15 theorem
 c. BDDC
 d. BIBO stability

18. In probability theory and statistics, the _____ (or expectation value or mean and for continuous random variables with a density function it is the probability density -weighted integral of the possible values.

The term '_____' can be misleading.

 a. ALGOR
 b. ACTRAN
 c. AUSM
 d. Expected value

19. In calculus, the _____ states, roughly, that given a section of a smooth curve, there is at least one point on that section at which the derivative (slope) of the curve is equal (parallel) to the 'average' derivative of the section. It is used to prove theorems that make global conclusions about a function on an interval starting from local hypotheses about derivatives at points of the interval.

This theorem can be understood concretely by applying it to motion: If a car travels one hundred miles in one hour, so its average speed during that time was 100 miles per hour.

 a. First derivative test
 b. Leibniz differential
 c. Fresnel integrals
 d. Mean Value Theorem

20. The _____ is a method of finding the area of a shape by inscribing inside it a sequence of polygons whose areas converge to the area of the containing shape. If the sequence is correctly constructed, the difference in area between the nth polygon and the containing shape will become arbitrarily small as n becomes large. As this difference becomes arbitrarily small, the possible values for the area of the shape are systematically 'exhausted' by the lower bound areas successively established by the sequence members.

 a. BDDC
 b. BIBO stability
 c. 15 theorem
 d. Method of exhaustion

21. A _____ or Gompertz function, named after Benjamin Gompertz, is a sigmoid function. It is a type of mathematical model for a time series, where growth is slowest at the start and end of a time period. Graphs of Gompertz curves, showing the effect of varying one of a,b,c while keeping the others constant.

$$y(t) = ae^{be^{ct}}$$

where

- a is the upper asymptote
- c is the growth rate
- b, c are negative numbers
- e is Euler's Number (e = 2.71828...)

The function curve can be derived from Gompertz's law, which states the rate of mortality (decay) falls exponentially with current size. Mathematically

$$k^r \propto \frac{1}{y(t)}$$

where

- $r = \dfrac{y'(t)}{y(t)}$ is the rate of growth.
- k is an arbitrary constant.

Examples of uses for Gompertz curves include:

- Mobile phone uptake, where costs were initially high (so uptake was slow), followed by a period of rapid growth, followed by a slowing of uptake as saturation was reached.
- Population in a confined space, as birth rates first increase and then slow as resource limits are reached.
- Modeling of growth of tumors

In the sixties A.K. Laird for the first time successfully used the _____ to fit data of growth of tumors. In fact, tumors are cellular populations growing in a confined space where the availability of nutrients is limited.

a. Gompertz curve
c. Neumann-Dirichlet method
b. Spheroidal wave functions
d. Duffing equation

22. In calculus, the _____ is a theorem regarding the limit of a function.

The _____ is a technical result which is very important in proofs in calculus and mathematical analysis. It is typically used to confirm the limit of a function via comparison with two other functions whose limits are known or easily computed.

a. 15 theorem
c. Limit of a sequence
b. Table of limits
d. Squeeze Theorem

23. In mathematics and computer science, the floor and ceiling functions map a real number to the next smallest or next largest integer. More precisely, floor(x) is the largest integer not greater than x and ceiling(x) is the smallest integer not less than x.

The _____ is also called the greatest integer or entier function, and the floor of a nonnegative x may be called the integral part or integral value of x. Computer languages (other than APL) commonly use ENTIER(x) (Algol), floor(x), or int(x) (C and C++).

a. Hyperbolic functions
c. Floor function
b. Signum function
d. Hyperbolic tangent

24. In calculus, the _____ allows you to take constants outside a derivative and concentrate on differentiating the function of x itself. This is a part of the linearity of differentiation.

Suppose you have a function

$$g(x) = k \cdot f(x).$$

where k is a constant.

Use the formula for differentiation from first principles to obtain:

$$g'(x) = \lim_{h \to 0} \frac{g(x+h) - g(x)}{h}$$
$$g'(x) = \lim_{h \to 0} \frac{k \cdot f(x+h) - k \cdot f(x)}{h}$$
$$g'(x) = \lim_{h \to 0} \frac{k(f(x+h) - f(x))}{h}$$
$$g'(x) = k \lim_{h \to 0} \frac{f(x+h) - f(x)}{h} \quad (*)$$
$$g'(x) = k \cdot f'(x).$$

This is the statement of the _____, in Lagrange's notation for differentiation.

a. Differentiation rules
c. Product rule
b. Reciprocal Rule
d. Constant factor rule in differentiation

Chapter 2. LIMITS AND DERIVATIVES

25. Continuous functions are of utmost importance in mathematics and applications. However, not all functions are continuous. If a function is not continuous at a point in its domain, one says that it has a _____ there. The set of all points of _____ of a function may be a discrete set, a dense set, or even the entire domain of the function.
   - a. BIBO stability
   - b. 15 theorem
   - c. BDDC
   - d. Discontinuity

26. In mathematics, a _____ is a function for which, intuitively, small changes in the input result in small changes in the output. Otherwise, a function is said to be discontinuous. A _____ with a continuous inverse function is called bicontinuous. An intuitive though imprecise (and inexact) idea of continuity is given by the common statement that a _____ is a function whose graph can be drawn without lifting the chalk from the blackboard.
   - a. Maxima
   - b. Leibniz function
   - c. Continuous function
   - d. Dirichlet integral

27. In mathematical analysis, the _____ states that for each value between the least upper bound and greatest lower bound of the image of a continuous function there is a corresponding value in its domain mapping to the original. _____

   - Version I. The _____ states the following: If the function y = f(x) is continuous on the interval [a, b], and u is a number between f(a) and f(b), then there is a c ∈ [a, b] such that f(c) = u.

   - Version II. Suppose that I is an interval [a, b] in the real numbers R and that f : I → R is a continuous function. Then the image set f(I) is also an interval, and either it contains [f(a), f(b)], or it contains [f(b), f(a)]; that is,

      f(I) ⊇ [f(a), f(b)], or f(I) ⊇ [f(b), f(a)].

It is frequently stated in the following equivalent form: Suppose that f : [a, b] → R is continuous and that u is a real number satisfying f(a) < u < f(b) or f(a) > u > f(b).) Then for some c ∈ [a, b], f(c) = u.

This captures an intuitive property of continuous functions: given f continuous on [1, 2], if f(1) = 3 and f(2) = 5 then f must take the value 4 somewhere between 1 and 2.

   - a. ACTRAN
   - b. ALGOR
   - c. Intermediate Value Theorem
   - d. AUSM

28. In calculus, the _____ is a shorthand method of finding the derivative of a function that is the reciprocal of a differentiable function, without using the quotient rule or chain rule.

The _____ states that the derivative of 1 / g(x) is given by

$$\frac{d}{dx}\left(\frac{1}{g(x)}\right) = \frac{-g'(x)}{(g(x))^2}$$

where $g(x) \neq 0$.

The _____ is derived from the quotient rule, with the numerator f(x) = 1. Then,

It is also possible to derive the _____ from the chain rule, by a process very much like that of the derivation of the quotient rule.

   a. Constant factor rule in differentiation   b. Reciprocal Rule
   c. Quotient Rule   d. Differentiation rules

29. Suppose f is a function. Then the line y = a is a _____ for f if

$$\lim_{x \to \infty} f(x) = a \text{ or } \lim_{x \to -\infty} f(x) = a.$$

Intuitively, this means that f(x) can be made as close as desired to a by making x big enough. How big is big enough depends on how close one wishes to make f(x) to a.

   a. Bounded function   b. Mountain pass theorem
   c. Vertical asymptote   d. Horizontal asymptote

30. In calculus, a branch of mathematics, the _____ is a measurement of how a function changes when its input changes. Loosely speaking, a _____ can be thought of as how much a quantity is changing at some given point. For example, the _____ of the position (or distance) of a vehicle with respect to time is the instantaneous velocity (respectively, instantaneous speed) at which the vehicle is traveling.

The process of finding a _____ is called differentiation. The fundamental theorem of calculus states that differentiation is the reverse process to integration.

   a. Ramp function   b. Derivative
   c. Concave upwards   d. Mountain pass theorem

31. In mathematics, a (topological) _____ is defined as follows: let I be an interval of real numbers (i.e. a non-empty connected subset of $\mathbb{R}$); then a _____ γ is a continuous mapping $\gamma : I \to X$, where X is a topological space. The _____ γ is said to be simple if it is injective, i.e. if for all x, y in I, we have $\gamma(x) = \gamma(y) \implies x = y$. If I is a closed bounded interval $[a, b]$, we also allow the possibility $\gamma(a) = \gamma(b)$ (this convention makes it possible to talk about closed simple _____.)

   a. Curve   b. Closed curve
   c. Tractrix   d. Prolate cycloid

32. This article will state and prove the _____ for differentiation, and then use it to prove these two formulas.

The _____ for differentiation states that for every natural number n, the derivative of $f(x) = x^n$ is $f'(x) = nx^{n-1}$, that is,

$$(x^n)' = nx^{n-1}.$$

The _____ for integration

$$\int x^n \, dx = \frac{x^{n+1}}{n+1} + C$$

for natural n is then an easy consequence. One just needs to take the derivative of this equality and use the _____ and linearity of differentiation on the right-hand side.

   a. Limits of integration   b. Hyperbolic angle
   c. Dirichlet integral   d. Power Rule

33. In mathematics, the _____ (or replacement set) of a given function is the set of 'input' values for which the function is defined. For instance, the _____ of cosine would be all real numbers, while the _____ of the square root would be only numbers greater than or equal to 0 (ignoring complex numbers in both cases.) In a representation of a function in a xy Cartesian coordinate system, the _____ is represented on the x axis (or abscissa.)
   a. BDDC   b. BIBO stability
   c. 15 theorem   d. Domain

34. In calculus, _____, was originally the use of expressions such as dx and dy and to represent 'infinitely small' (or infinitesimal) increments of quantities x and y, just as >Δx and >Δy represent finite increments of x and y respectively. So for y being a function of x, or

the derivative of y with respect to x, which later came to be viewed as

was, according to Leibniz, the quotient of an infinitesimal increment of y by an infinitesimal increment of x, or

where the right hand side is Lagrange's notation for the derivative of f at x.

Similarly, although mathematicians usually now view an integral

as a limit

where >Δx is an interval containing x_i, Leibniz viewed it as the sum (the integral sign denoting summation) of infinitely many infinitesimal quantities f(x) dx.

    a. Notation for differentiation   b. Fermat differentiation
    c. Leibniz's notation   d. Gradient

35. In mathematics, a differential operator is an operator defined as a function of the _____. It is helpful, as a matter of notation first, to consider differentiation as an abstract operation, accepting a function and returning another (in the style of a higher-order function in computer science.)

There are certainly reasons not to restrict to linear operators; for instance the Schwarzian derivative is a well-known non-linear operator.

    a. Second partial derivatives test   b. Surface integral
    c. Vector Laplacian   d. Differentiation operator

36. The _____ is a test to determine if a relation or its graph is a function or not. For a relation or graph to be a function, it can have at most a single y-value for each x-value. Thus, a vertical line drawn at any x-position on the graph of a function will intersect the graph at most once.
    a. 15 theorem   b. Vertical Line Test
    c. BIBO stability   d. BDDC

37. Let f be a differentiable function, and let f'(x) be its derivative. The derivative of f'(x) (if it has one) is written f''(x) and is called the _____ of f. Similarly, the derivative of a _____, if it exists, is written f'''(x) and is called the third derivative of f.
    a. Stationary phase approximation   b. Horizontal asymptote
    c. Ramp function   d. Second derivative

38. In physics, and more specifically kinematics, _____ is the change in velocity over time. Because velocity is a vector, it can change in two ways: a change in magnitude and/or a change in direction. In one dimension, _____ is the rate at which something speeds up or slows down.
    a. ALGOR   b. ACTRAN
    c. AUSM   d. Acceleration

39. Let f be a differentiable function, and let f'(x) be its derivative. The derivative of f'(x) (if it has one) is written f''(x) and is called the second derivative of f. Similarly, the derivative of a second derivative, if it exists, is written f'''(x) and is called the _____ of f.
    a. Third derivative
    b. Semi-differentiability
    c. Geometric function theory
    d. Second derivative

Chapter 3. DIFFERENTIATION RULES

1. In mathematics, a _____ is a function whose values do not vary and thus are constant. For example, if we have the function f(x) = 4, then f is constant since f maps any value to 4. More formally, a function f : A → B is a _____ if f(x) = f(y) for all x and y in A.

    a. Piecewise-defined function
    b. Range
    c. Surjective
    d. Constant function

2. This article will state and prove the _____ for differentiation, and then use it to prove these two formulas.

The _____ for differentiation states that for every natural number n, the derivative of $f(x) = x^n$ is $f'(x) = nx^{n-1}$, that is,

$$(x^n)' = nx^{n-1}.$$

The _____ for integration

$$\int x^n \, dx = \frac{x^{n+1}}{n+1} + C$$

for natural n is then an easy consequence. One just needs to take the derivative of this equality and use the _____ and linearity of differentiation on the right-hand side.

    a. Hyperbolic angle
    b. Dirichlet integral
    c. Limits of integration
    d. Power Rule

3. In the two-dimensional case, a _____ perpendicularly intersects the tangent line to a curve at a given point.

The _____ is often used in computer graphics to determine a surface's orientation toward a light source for flat shading, or the orientation of each of the corners (vertices) to mimic a curved surface with Phong shading.

For a polygon (such as a triangle), a surface normal can be calculated as the vector cross product of two (non-parallel) edges of the polygon.

    a. PDE surfaces
    b. Prolate
    c. Parametric surface
    d. Normal line

4. In calculus, the _____ allows you to take constants outside a derivative and concentrate on differentiating the function of x itself. This is a part of the linearity of differentiation.

Suppose you have a function

$$g(x) = k \cdot f(x).$$

where k is a constant.

Chapter 3. DIFFERENTIATION RULES

Use the formula for differentiation from first principles to obtain:

$$g'(x) = \lim_{h \to 0} \frac{g(x+h) - g(x)}{h}$$
$$g'(x) = \lim_{h \to 0} \frac{k \cdot f(x+h) - k \cdot f(x)}{h}$$
$$g'(x) = \lim_{h \to 0} \frac{k(f(x+h) - f(x))}{h}$$
$$g'(x) = k \lim_{h \to 0} \frac{f(x+h) - f(x)}{h} \quad (*)$$
$$g'(x) = k \cdot f'(x).$$

This is the statement of the _____, in Lagrange's notation for differentiation.

a. Differentiation rules
b. Product rule
c. Reciprocal Rule
d. Constant factor rule in differentiation

5. In mathematics, an _____ is an infinite series of the form

$$\sum_{n=0}^{\infty} (-1)^n a_n,$$

with $a_n \geq 0$ (or $a_n \leq 0$) for all n. A finite sum of this kind is an alternating sum. An _____ converges if the terms a_n converge to 0 monotonically.

a. Extreme value
b. Uniform convergence
c. Alternating Series
d. Infinite series

6. In mathematics, a _____ is a function which preserves the given order. This concept first arose in calculus, and was later generalized to the more abstract setting of order theory.

In calculus, a function f defined on a subset of the real numbers with real values is called monotonic (also monotonically increasing or non-decreasing), if for all x and y such that x >≤ y one has f(x) >≤ f(y), so f preserves the order.

a. 15 theorem
b. Monotonic function
c. Pseudo-differential operator
d. Pettis integral

7. In mathematics, a _____ is an ordered list of objects (or events). Like a set, it contains members (also called elements or terms), and the number of terms (possibly infinite) is called the length of the _____. Unlike a set, order matters, and the exact same elements can appear multiple times at different positions in the _____.

a. Y-intercept
c. 15 theorem
b. Sequence
d. BDDC

8. In calculus, a branch of mathematics, the _____ is a measurement of how a function changes when its input changes. Loosely speaking, a _____ can be thought of as how much a quantity is changing at some given point. For example, the _____ of the position (or distance) of a vehicle with respect to time is the instantaneous velocity (respectively, instantaneous speed) at which the vehicle is traveling.

The process of finding a _____ is called differentiation. The fundamental theorem of calculus states that differentiation is the reverse process to integration.

a. Ramp function
c. Mountain pass theorem
b. Concave upwards
d. Derivative

9. The _____ is a function in mathematics. The application of this function to a value x is written as exp(x). Equivalently, this can be written in the form e^x, where e is a mathematical constant, the base of the natural logarithm, which equals approximately 2.718281828, and is also known as Euler's number.

a. Area hyperbolic functions
c. Integral part
b. ACTRAN
d. Exponential function

10. In mathematics, the concept of a '_____' is used to describe the behavior of a function as its argument or input either 'gets close' to some point, or as the argument becomes arbitrarily large; or the behavior of a sequence's elements as their index increases indefinitely. Limits are used in calculus and other branches of mathematical analysis to define derivatives and continuity.

In formulas, _____ is usually abbreviated as lim

a. 15 theorem
c. Limit
b. BIBO stability
d. BDDC

11. In calculus, the _____ is a formula used to find the derivatives of products of functions. It may be stated thus:

$$(f \cdot g)' = f' \cdot g + f \cdot g'$$

or in the Leibniz notation thus:

$$\frac{d}{dx}(u \cdot v) = u \cdot \frac{dv}{dx} + v \cdot \frac{du}{dx}.$$

Discovery of this rule is credited to Gottfried Leibniz, who demonstrated it using differentials. Here is Leibniz's argument: Let u and v be two differentiable functions of x.

a. Product Rule
c. Quotient Rule
b. Constant factor rule in differentiation
d. Reciprocal Rule

Chapter 3. DIFFERENTIATION RULES

12. In calculus, the _____ is a method of finding the derivative of a function that is the quotient of two other functions for which derivatives exist.

If the function one wishes to differentiate, f(x), can be written as

$$f(x) = \frac{g(x)}{h(x)}$$

and h(x) ≠ 0, then the rule states that the derivative of g(x) / h(x) is equal to:

$$\frac{d}{dx}f(x) = f'(x) = \frac{g'(x)h(x) - g(x)h'(x)}{[h(x)]^2}.$$

Or, more precisely, if all x in some open set containing the number a satisfy h(x) ≠ 0; and g'(a) and h'(a) both exist; then, f'(a) exists as well and:

$$f'(a) = \frac{g'(a)h(a) - g(a)h'(a)}{[h(a)]^2}.$$

The derivative of (4x − 2) / (x² + 1) is:

$$\frac{d}{dx}\left[\frac{(4x-2)}{x^2+1}\right] = \frac{(x^2+1)(4) - (4x-2)(2x)}{(x^2+1)^2}$$
$$= \frac{(4x^2+4) - (8x^2-4x)}{(x^2+1)^2} \qquad = \frac{-4x^2+4x+4}{(x^2+1)^2}$$

In the example above, the choices

g(x) = 4x − 2
h(x) = x² + 1

were made. Analogously, the derivative of sin(x) / x² (when x ≠ 0) is:

$$\frac{\cos(x)x^2 - \sin(x)2x}{x^4}$$

Another example is:

$$f(x) = \frac{2x^2}{x^3}$$

whereas g(x) = 2x² and h(x) = x³, and g'(x) = 4x and h'(x) = 3x².

a. Reciprocal Rule
b. Differentiation rules
c. Product rule
d. Quotient Rule

13. In mathematics, the _____ , is the curve defined as follows.

Starting with a fixed circle, a point O on the circle is chosen. For any other point A on the circle, the secant line OA is drawn. The point M is diametrically opposite O. The line OA intersects the tangent at M at the point N. The line parallel to OM through N, and the line perpendicular to OM through A intersect at P. As the point A is varied, the path of P is the witch.

a. Folium of Descartes
b. Cochleoid
c. Witch of Agnesi
d. Closed curve

14. In calculus, the _____ is a shorthand method of finding the derivative of a function that is the reciprocal of a differentiable function, without using the quotient rule or chain rule.

The _____ states that the derivative of 1 / g(x) is given by

$$\frac{d}{dx}\left(\frac{1}{g(x)}\right) = \frac{-g'(x)}{(g(x))^2}$$

where $g(x) \neq 0$.

The _____ is derived from the quotient rule, with the numerator f(x) = 1. Then,

It is also possible to derive the _____ from the chain rule, by a process very much like that of the derivation of the quotient rule.

a. Constant factor rule in differentiation
b. Differentiation rules
c. Quotient Rule
d. Reciprocal Rule

15. In mathematics, the _____ is a way to approximately calculate the definite integral

Chapter 3. DIFFERENTIATION RULES

$$\int_a^b f(x)\,dx.$$

The _____ works by approximating the region under the graph of the function f by a trapezoid and calculating its area. It follows that

$$\int_a^b f(x)\,dx \approx (b-a)\frac{f(a)+f(b)}{2}.$$

To calculate this integral more accurately, one first splits the interval of integration [a,b] into n smaller subintervals, and then applies the _____ on each of them. One obtains the composite _____:

$$\int_a^b f(x)\,dx \approx \frac{b-a}{n}\left[\frac{f(a)+f(b)}{2} + \sum_{k=1}^{n-1} f\left(a+k\frac{b-a}{n}\right)\right].$$

This can alternatively be written as:

$$\int_a^b f(x)\,dx \approx \frac{b-a}{2n}\left(f(x_0)+2f(x_1)+2f(x_2)+\cdots+2f(x_{n-1})+f(x_n)\right)$$

where

$$x_k = a + k\frac{b-a}{n}, \text{ for } k=0,1,\ldots,n$$

(one can also use a non-uniform grid.)

- a. BDDC
- b. Trapezoidal Rule
- c. 15 theorem
- d. BIBO stability

16. Trigonometry is a branch of mathematics that deals with triangles, particularly those plane triangles in which one angle has 90 degrees (right triangles.) Trigonometry deals with relationships between the sides and the angles of triangles and with the _____ functions, which describe those relationships.

Trigonometry has applications in both pure mathematics and in applied mathematics, where it is essential in many branches of science and technology.

- a. 15 theorem
- b. Trigonometric functions
- c. Trigonometric integrals
- d. Trigonometric

Chapter 3. DIFFERENTIATION RULES

17. In mathematics, the _____ are functions of an angle. They are important in the study of triangles and modeling periodic phenomena, among many other applications. _____ are commonly defined as ratios of two sides of a right triangle containing the angle, and can equivalently be defined as the lengths of various line segments from a unit circle.

   a. 15 theorem
   b. Trigonometric integrals
   c. Trigonometric
   d. Trigonometric functions

18. In mathematics, the _____ is a criterion for the convergence (a convergence test) of an infinite series

$$\sum_{n=1}^{\infty} a_n.$$

It is particularly useful in connection with power series.

The _____ was developed first by Cauchy and so is sometimes known as the Cauchy _____ or Cauchy's radical test. The _____ uses the number

$$C = \limsup_{n \to \infty} \sqrt[n]{|a_n|},$$

where 'lim sup' denotes the limit superior, possibly ∞.

   a. Binomial series
   b. Root Test
   c. Related rates
   d. Dirichlet integral

19. In mathematics, a _____ is a constant multiplicative factor of a certain object. For example, in the expression $9x^2$, the _____ of x^2 is 9.

The object can be such things as a variable, a vector, a function, etc.

   a. Leading coefficient
   b. Degree of the polynomial
   c. Coefficient
   d. Difference polynomial

20. In a totally ordered set all elements are mutually comparable, so such a set can have at most one minimal element and at most one maximal element. Then, due to mutual comparability, the minimal element will also be the least element and the maximal element will also be the greatest element. Thus in a totally ordered set we can simply use the terms minimum and _____.

   a. Maximum
   b. Complex analysis
   c. Hyperbolic angle
   d. Dirichlet integral

21. In calculus, the _____ is a formula for the derivative of the composite of two functions.

Chapter 3. DIFFERENTIATION RULES

In intuitive terms, if a variable, y, depends on a second variable, u, which in turn depends on a third variable, x, then the rate of change of y with respect to x can be computed as the rate of change of y with respect to u multiplied by the rate of change of u with respect to x. Schematically,

$$\frac{dy}{dx} = \frac{dy}{du} \cdot \frac{du}{dx}.$$

a. Differentiation rules
b. Quotient Rule
c. Reciprocal Rule
d. Chain Rule

22. In mathematics, a _____ represents the application of one function to the results of another. For instance, the functions f: X → Y and g: Y → Z can be composed by first computing f(x) and then applying a function g to the output of f(x).

Thus one obtains a function g ∘ f: X → Z defined by (g ∘ f)(x) = g(f(x)) for all x in X. The notation g ∘ f is read as 'g circle f', or 'g composed with f', 'g after f', 'g following f', or just 'g of f'.

a. Surjective
b. Constant function
c. Range
d. Composite function

23. In mathematics, a _____ is a unicursal quartic curve with three inflection points, given by the equation

$$a^2 y^2 - b^2 x^2 = x^2 y^2$$

The bullet curve has three double points in the real projective plane, at x=0 and y=0, x=0 and z=0, and y=0 and z=0, and is therefore a unicursal (rational) curve of genus zero.

If

$$f(z) = \sum_{n=0}^{\infty} \binom{2n}{n} z^{2n+1} = z + 2z^3 + 6z^5 + 20z^7 + \cdots$$

then

$$y = f\left(\frac{x}{2a}\right) \pm 2b$$

are the two branches of the bullet curve at the origin.

a. Folium of Descartes
b. Closed curve
c. Hypocycloid
d. Bullet-nose curve

24. In mathematics, a (topological) _____ is defined as follows: let I be an interval of real numbers (i.e. a non-empty connected subset of $\mathbb{R}$); then a _____ γ is a continuous mapping $\gamma : I \to X$, where X is a topological space. The _____ γ is said to be simple if it is injective, i.e. if for all x, y in I, we have $\gamma(x) = \gamma(y) \implies x = y$. If I is a closed bounded interval $[a, b]$, we also allow the possibility $\gamma(a) = \gamma(b)$ (this convention makes it possible to talk about closed simple _____.)

    a. Closed curve
    b. Tractrix
    c. Prolate cycloid
    d. Curve

25. The _____ is a plane fractal first described by Waclaw Sierpinski in 1916. The carpet is a generalization of the Cantor set to two dimensions (another is Cantor dust.) Sierpinski demonstrated that this fractal is a universal curve, in that any possible one-dimensional graph, projected onto the two-dimensional plane, is homeomorphic to a subset of the _____.

    a. Siegel disc
    b. Sierpinski carpet
    c. BDDC
    d. 15 theorem

26. In acoustics and telecommunication, a _____ of a wave is a component frequency of the signal that is an integer multiple of the fundamental frequency. For example, if the fundamental frequency is f, the harmonics have frequencies f, 2f, 3f, 4f, etc. The harmonics have the property that they are all periodic at the fundamental frequency, therefore the sum of harmonics is also periodic at that frequency.

    a. BDDC
    b. 15 theorem
    c. BIBO stability
    d. Harmonic

27. _____ is the motion of a simple harmonic oscillator, a motion that is neither driven nor damped. The motion is periodic - as it repeats itself at standard intervals in a specific manner - and sinusoidal, with constant amplitude; the acceleration of a body executing _____ is directly proportional to the displacement of the body from the equilibrium position and is always directed towards the equilibrium position.

The motion is characterized by its amplitude (which is always positive), its period, the time for a single oscillation, its frequency, the reciprocal of the period (i.e. the number of cycles per unit time), and its phase, which determines the starting point on the sine wave.

    a. BDDC
    b. 15 theorem
    c. Holonomic
    d. Simple harmonic motion

28. In calculus, a method called _____ can be applied to implicitly defined functions. This method is an application of the chain rule allowing one to calculate the derivative of a function given implicitly.

As explained in the introduction, y can be given as a function of x implicitly rather than explicitly. When we have an equation R (x,y) = 0, we may be able to solve it for y and then differentiate. However, sometimes it is simpler to differentiate R(x,y) with respect to x and then solve for dy / dx.

    a. Automatic differentiation
    b. Ordinary differential equation
    c. Implicit function
    d. Implicit differentiation

Chapter 3. DIFFERENTIATION RULES

29. In mathematics, an _____ is a generalization for the concept of a function in which the dependent variable has not been given 'explicitly' in terms of the independent variable. To give a function f explicitly is to provide a prescription for determining the output value of the function y in terms of the input value x:

$$y = f(x.)$$

By contrast, the function is implicit if the value of y is obtained from x by solving an equation of the form:

$$R(x,y) = 0.$$

a. Implicit differentiation
b. Ordinary differential equation
c. Implicit function
d. Automatic differentiation

30. In Geometry, the _____ is an algebraic curve defined by the equation

$$x^3 + y^3 - 3axy = 0$$

It forms a loop in the first quadrant with a double point at the origin and asymptote

$$x + y + a = 0$$

It is symmetrical about y = x.

a. Cochleoid
b. Prolate cycloid
c. Folium of Descartes
d. Curve

31. The _____ are a pair of first order, non-linear, differential equations frequently used to describe the dynamics of biological systems in which two species interact, one a predator and one its prey. They were proposed independently by Alfred J. Lotka in 1925 and Vito Volterra in 1926.

where

- y is the number of some predator;
- x is the number of its prey;
- dy/dt and dx/dt represents the growth of the two populations against time;
- t represents the time; and
- >α, >β, >γ and >δ are parameters representing the interaction of the two species.

Chapter 3. DIFFERENTIATION RULES

When multiplied out, the equations take a form useful for physical interpretation. Their origin should be considered from a more general framework,

where both functions represent per capita growth rates of the prey and predator, respectively.

a. BDDC
b. 15 theorem
c. BIBO stability
d. Lotka-Volterra equations

32. The largest and the smallest element of a set are called extreme values, absolute extrema, or extreme records.

For a differentiable function f, if $f(x_0)$ is an _____ for the set of all values f(x), and if x_0 is in the interior of the domain of f, then x_0 is a critical point, by Fermat's theorem.

In the case of a general partial order one should not confuse a least element (smaller than all other) and a minimal element (nothing is smaller.)

a. Integration by substitution
b. Infinitesimal
c. Extreme Value Theorem
d. Extreme Value

33. In calculus, the _____ states that if a real-valued function f is continuous in the closed and bounded interval [a,b], then f must attain its maximum and minimum value, each at least once. That is, there exist numbers c and d in [a,b] such that:

A related theorem is the boundedness theorem which states that a continuous function f in the closed interval [a,b] is bounded on that interval. That is, there exist real numbers m and M such that:

The _____ enriches the boundedness theorem by saying that not only is the function bounded, but it also attains its least upper bound as its maximum and its greatest lower bound as its minimum.

a. Uniform convergence
b. Infinitesimal
c. Integral of secant cubed
d. Extreme Value Theorem

Chapter 3. DIFFERENTIATION RULES

34. In mathematics, the _____ of a function y = f(x) is a function that, in some fashion, 'undoes' the effect of f The _____ of f is denoted f $^{-1}$. The statements y=f(x) and x=f $^{-1}$(y) are equivalent.
   a. ACTRAN
   b. ALGOR
   c. Inverse
   d. AUSM

35. In mathematics, the _____ or cyclometric functions are the inverse functions of the trigonometric functions. The principal inverses are listed in the following table.

If x is allowed to be a complex number, then the range of y applies only to its real part.

   a. ACTRAN
   b. AUSM
   c. Inverse trigonometric functions
   d. ALGOR

36. In mathematics, the _____, introduced by German mathematician Georg Cantor in 1883 (but discovered in 1875 by Henry John Stephen Smith), is a set of points lying on a single line segment that has a number of remarkable and deep properties. Through consideration of it, Cantor and others helped lay the foundations of modern general topology. Although Cantor himself defined the set in a general, abstract way, the most common modern construction is the Cantor ternary set, built by removing the middle thirds of a line segment.
   a. 15 theorem
   b. BDDC
   c. Planar Lamina
   d. Cantor set

37. The _____ is a curve, with a Cartesian equation of

$$x^4 = x^2 + y^2 ,$$

or, in polar coordinates,

$$r = \sec^2 \theta .$$

This quartic curve was studied by the Greek astronomer and mathematician Eudoxus of Cnidus (c. 408 BC - c.347 BC) in relation to the classical problem of doubling the cube.

- List of curves

   a. Dolbeault operator
   b. Tschirnhausen cubic
   c. Kampyle of Eudoxus
   d. Macbeath surface

38. In calculus, _____, was originally the use of expressions such as dx and dy and to represent 'infinitely small' (or infinitesimal) increments of quantities x and y, just as >Δx and >Δy represent finite increments of x and y respectively. So for y being a function of x, or

the derivative of y with respect to x, which later came to be viewed as

was, according to Leibniz, the quotient of an infinitesimal increment of y by an infinitesimal increment of x, or

where the right hand side is Lagrange's notation for the derivative of f at x.

Similarly, although mathematicians usually now view an integral

as a limit

where >Δx is an interval containing x_i, Leibniz viewed it as the sum (the integral sign denoting summation) of infinitely many infinitesimal quantities f(x) dx.

a. Leibniz's notation
c. Notation for differentiation
b. Fermat differentiation
d. Gradient

39. In mathematics, a _____ is the graph of the system of parametric equations

$$x = A\sin(at + \delta), \quad y = B\sin(bt),$$

which describes complex harmonic motion. This family of curves was investigated by Nathaniel Bowditch in 1815, and later in more detail by Jules Antoine Lissajous in 1857.

The appearance of the figure is highly sensitive to the ratio a/b.

a. BIBO stability
c. 15 theorem
b. BDDC
d. Lissajous curve

Chapter 3. DIFFERENTIATION RULES

40. In mathematics, an _____ is a particular type of curve: a hypocycloid with four cusps. Astroids are also superellipses: all astroids are scaled versions of the curve specified by the equation

$$x^{2/3} + y^{2/3} = 1$$

Its modern name comes from the Greek word for 'star'.

 a. ACTRAN
 c. Epicycloid
 b. ALGOR
 d. Astroid

41. A _____ is closed curve with one cusp.

In geometry, the _____ is an epicycloid with one cusp.

Rolling circle around another fixed circle produces _____ (red curve) Conformal mapping from circle to _____

- epicycloid produced as the path (or locus) of a point on the circumference of a circle as that circle rolls around another fixed circle with the same radius.

- limaçon with one cusp. The cusp is formed when the ratio of a to b in the equation is equal to one.

 a. BDDC
 c. 15 theorem
 b. BIBO stability
 d. Cardioid

42. In mathematics, an _____, is the apparent shape of a circle viewed obliquely from outside it, as distinct from a hyperbola which is the shape seen from inside. It is the finite or bounded case of a conic section as a shape cut in a cone by a plane, the unbounded cases being the parabola, which like the _____ remains connected, and the hyperbola, which separates into two connected components or branches.

Equivalently an _____ can be defined as the locus of points, or path traced out, in a plane such that the sum of the distances from the moving point to two fixed points remains constant.

 a. ACTRAN
 c. ALGOR
 b. AUSM
 d. Ellipse

43. The _____, named after the mathematician Ehrenfried Walther von Tschirnhaus, is a plane curve which is defined by either of these formulae:

$y^2 = x^3 + 3x^2$

$a = r\cos^3(\theta / 3.)$

Chapter 3. DIFFERENTIATION RULES

    a. Dolbeault operator
    b. Strophoid
    c. Kampyle of Eudoxus
    d. Tschirnhausen cubic

44. In mathematics, two vectors are _____ if they are perpendicular, i.e., they form a right angle. For example, a subway and the street above, although they do not physically intersect, are _____ if they cross at a right angle.
    a. AUSM
    b. ALGOR
    c. Orthogonal
    d. ACTRAN

45. In mathematics, _____ are a family of curves in the plane that intersect a given family of curves at right angles. The problem is classical, but is now understood by means of complex analysis; see for example harmonic conjugate.

For a family of level curves described by g(x,y) = C, where C is a constant, the _____ may be found as the level curves of a new function f(x,y) by solving the partial differential equation

$$\nabla f \cdot \nabla g = 0$$

for f(x,y).

    a. AUSM
    b. ACTRAN
    c. Orthogonal trajectories
    d. ALGOR

46. A _____ is the path a moving object follows through space. The object might be a projectile or a satellite, for example. It thus includes the meaning of orbit - the path of a planet, an asteroid or a comet as it travels around a central mass.
    a. BIBO stability
    b. BDDC
    c. 15 theorem
    d. Trajectory

47. In mathematics, if f is a function from A to B then an _____ for f is a function in the opposite direction, from B to A, with the property that a round trip (a composition) from A to B to A (or from B to A to B) returns each element of the initial set to itself. Thus, if an input x into the function f produces an output y, then inputting y into the _____ f^{-1} (read f inverse, not to be confused with exponentiation) produces the output x. Not every function has an inverse; those that do are called invertible.
    a. Inverse function
    b. Augustin Louis Cauchy
    c. Aristotle
    d. Augustin-Jean Fresnel

48. The function $\log_b(x)$ depends on both b and x, but the term _____ in standard usage refers to a function of the form $\log_b(x)$ in which the base b is fixed and so the only argument is x. Thus there is one _____ for each value of the base b (which must be positive and must differ from 1.) Viewed in this way, the base-b _____ is the inverse function of the exponential function b^x.
    a. 15 theorem
    b. Logarithm function
    c. BIBO stability
    d. BDDC

49. In mathematics, specifically in calculus and complex analysis, the _____ of a function f is defined by the formula

Chapter 3. DIFFERENTIATION RULES

$$\frac{f'}{f}$$

where f ' is the derivative of f.

When f is a function f(x) of a real variable x, and takes real, strictly positive values, this is indeed the formula for (log f)', that is, the derivative of the natural logarithm of f, as follows directly from the chain rule.

Many properties of the real logarithm also apply to the _____, even when the function does not take values in the positive reals.

    a. Difference quotient
    b. Symmetric derivative
    c. Logarithmic derivative
    d. Linearity of differentiation

50. In physics, and more specifically kinematics, _____ is the change in velocity over time. Because velocity is a vector, it can change in two ways: a change in magnitude and/or a change in direction. In one dimension, _____ is the rate at which something speeds up or slows down.
    a. ACTRAN
    b. ALGOR
    c. AUSM
    d. Acceleration

51. In physics, _____ is defined as the rate of change of position. it is vector physical quantity; both speed and direction are required to define it. In the SI (metric) system, it is measured in meters per second: (m/s) or ms^{-1}.
    a. BDDC
    b. BIBO stability
    c. 15 theorem
    d. Velocity

52. The _____ of a material is defined as its mass per unit volume. The symbol of _____ is ρ '>rho.)

Mathematically:

$$d = \frac{m}{V}$$

where:

    d is the _____,
    m is the mass,
    V is the volume.

    a. Density
    b. BDDC
    c. 15 theorem
    d. BIBO stability

Chapter 3. DIFFERENTIATION RULES

53. _____, linear mass density or linear mass is a measure of mass per unit of length, and it is a characteristic of strings or other one-dimensional objects. The SI unit of _____ is the kilogram per metre (kg/m.) The _____, μ (sometimes denoted by λ), of an object is defined as:

$$\mu = \frac{\partial m}{\partial x}$$

where m is the mass, and x is a coordinate along the (one dimensional) object.

a. BDDC
b. 15 theorem
c. BIBO stability
d. Linear density

54. In mathematical analysis, the _____ states that for each value between the least upper bound and greatest lower bound of the image of a continuous function there is a corresponding value in its domain mapping to the original. _____

- Version I. The _____ states the following: If the function y = f(x) is continuous on the interval [a, b], and u is a number between f(a) and f(b), then there is a c ∈ [a, b] such that f(c) = u.

- Version II. Suppose that I is an interval [a, b] in the real numbers R and that f : I → R is a continuous function. Then the image set f(I) is also an interval, and either it contains [f(a), f(b)], or it contains [f(b), f(a)]; that is,

    f(I) ⊇ [f(a), f(b)], or f(I) ⊇ [f(b), f(a)].

It is frequently stated in the following equivalent form: Suppose that f : [a, b] → R is continuous and that u is a real number satisfying f(a) < u < f(b) or f(a) > u > f(b.) Then for some c ∈ [a, b], f(c) = u.

This captures an intuitive property of continuous functions: given f continuous on [1, 2], if f(1) = 3 and f(2) = 5 then f must take the value 4 somewhere between 1 and 2.

a. ALGOR
b. Intermediate Value Theorem
c. ACTRAN
d. AUSM

55. An _____ process is a change in which the temperature of the system stays constant: ΔT = 0. This typically occurs when a system is in contact with an outside thermal reservoir (heat bath), and the change occurs slowly enough to allow the system to continually adjust to the temperature of the reservoir through heat exchange. An alternative special case in which a system exchanges no heat with its surroundings (Q = 0) is called an adiabatic process.

a. AUSM
b. ALGOR
c. ACTRAN
d. Isothermal

56. In elementary algebra, a _____ is a polynomial with two terms--the sum of two monomials--often bound by parenthesis or brackets when operated upon. It is the simplest kind of polynomial other than monomials.

- The _____ a² - b² can be factored as the product of two other binomials:

    a² - b² = (a + b)(a - b.)

    This is a special case of the more general formula:
    $$a^{n+1} - b^{n+1} = (a - b) \sum_{k=0}^{n} a^k b^{n-k}.$$

- The product of a pair of linear binomials (ax + b) and (cx + d) is:

    (ax + b)(cx + d) = acx² + axd + bcx + bd.

- A _____ raised to the nth power, represented as

    (a + b)^n

    can be expanded by means of the _____ theorem or, equivalently, using Pascal's triangle. Taking a simple example, the perfect square _____ (p + q)² can be found by squaring the first digit, adding twice the product of the first and second digit and finally adding the square of the second digit, to give p² + 2pq + q².

a. Partial fractions
b. Binomial
c. Multinomial theorem
d. Completing the square

57. In mathematics, the _____ is an important formula giving the expansion of powers of sums. Its simplest version states that

$$(x + y)^n = \sum_{k=0}^{n} \binom{n}{k} x^{n-k} y^k \qquad (1)$$

for any real or complex numbers x and y, and any non-negative integer n. The binomial coefficient appearing in (1) may be defined in terms of the factorial function n!:

$$\binom{n}{k} = \frac{n!}{k!(n-k)!}.$$

For example, here are the cases where 2 ≤ n ≤ 5:

$$(x + y)^2 = x^2 + 2xy + y^2$$
$$(x + y)^3 = x^3 + 3x^2y + 3xy^2 + y^3$$
$$(x + y)^4 = x^4 + 4x^3y + 6x^2y^2 + 4xy^3 + y^4$$
$$(x + y)^5 = x^5 + 5x^4y + 10x^3y^2 + 10x^2y^3 + 5xy^4 + y^5.$$

Formula (1) is valid more generally for any elements x and y of a semiring as long as xy = yx.

    a. Stirling transform
    c. Binomial Theorem
    b. Lah numbers
    d. Trinomial expansion

58. In mathematics, the simplest case of _____ refers to the study of problems in which one seeks to minimize or maximize a real function by systematically choosing the values of real or integer variables from within an allowed set. This (a scalar real valued objective function) is actually a small subset of this field which comprises a large area of applied mathematics and generalizes to study of means to obtain 'best available' values of some objective function given a defined domain where the elaboration is on the types of functions and the conditions and nature of the objects in the problem domain.

The first _____ technique, which is known as steepest descent, goes back to Gauss.

    a. ACTRAN
    c. AUSM
    b. ALGOR
    d. Optimization

59. In vector calculus, the _____ of a scalar field is a vector field which points in the direction of the greatest rate of increase of the scalar field, and whose magnitude is the greatest rate of change.

A generalization of the _____ for functions on a Euclidean space which have values in another Euclidean space is the Jacobian. A further generalization for a function from one Banach space to another is the Fréchet derivative.

    a. Leibniz's notation
    c. Smooth function
    b. Parametric derivative
    d. Gradient

60. In mathematics, the _____ is a representation of a function as an infinite sum of terms calculated from the values of its derivatives at a single point. It may be regarded as the limit of the Taylor polynomials. If the series is centered at zero, the series is also called a Maclaurin series.

    a. BIBO stability
    c. 15 theorem
    b. BDDC
    d. Taylor series

61. Jean Baptiste _____ (March 21, 1768 - May 16, 1830) was a French mathematician and physicist best known for initiating the investigation of Fourier series and their application to problems of heat flow. The Fourier transform is also named in his honour. Fourier is also generally credited with the discovery of the greenhouse effect.

    a. BIBO stability
    c. Joseph Fourier
    b. 15 theorem
    d. BDDC

Chapter 3. DIFFERENTIATION RULES

62. A _____ or Gompertz function, named after Benjamin Gompertz, is a sigmoid function. It is a type of mathematical model for a time series, where growth is slowest at the start and end of a time period. Graphs of Gompertz curves, showing the effect of varying one of a,b,c while keeping the others constant.

$$y(t) = ae^{be^{ct}}$$

where

- a is the upper asymptote
- c is the growth rate
- b, c are negative numbers
- e is Euler's Number (e = 2.71828...)

The function curve can be derived from Gompertz's law, which states the rate of mortality (decay) falls exponentially with current size. Mathematically

$$k^r \propto \frac{1}{y(t)}$$

where

- $r = \frac{y'(t)}{y(t)}$ is the rate of growth.
- k is an arbitrary constant.

Examples of uses for Gompertz curves include:

- Mobile phone uptake, where costs were initially high (so uptake was slow), followed by a period of rapid growth, followed by a slowing of uptake as saturation was reached.
- Population in a confined space, as birth rates first increase and then slow as resource limits are reached.
- Modeling of growth of tumors

In the sixties A.K. Laird for the first time successfully used the _____ to fit data of growth of tumors. In fact, tumors are cellular populations growing in a confined space where the availability of nutrients is limited.

a. Spheroidal wave functions
b. Neumann-Dirichlet method
c. Gompertz curve
d. Duffing equation

63. The mechanisms of _____; a point mass m_1 attracts another point mass m_2 by a force F_2 which is proportional to the product of the two masses and inversely proportional to the square of the distance (r) between them. Regardless of masses or distance, the magnitudes of $|F_1|$ and $|F_2|$ will always be equal. G is the gravitational constant.

_____ is an empirical physical law describing the gravitational attraction between bodies with mass.

Chapter 3. DIFFERENTIATION RULES

a. 15 theorem
b. BDDC
c. BIBO stability
d. Newton's law of universal gravitation

64. A quantity is said to be subject to _____ if it decreases at a rate proportional to its value. Symbolically, this can be expressed as the following differential equation, where N is the quantity and λ is a positive number called the decay constant.

$$\frac{dN}{dt} = -\lambda N.$$

The solution to this equation is:

$$N(t) = N_0 e^{-\lambda t}.$$

Here N(t) is the quantity at time t, and N_0 = N(0) is the initial quantity, i.e. the quantity at time t = 0.

a. Exponential decay
b. ALGOR
c. Exponential sum
d. ACTRAN

65. _____ (including exponential decay) occurs when the growth rate of a mathematical function is proportional to the function's current value. In the case of a discrete domain of definition with equal intervals it is also called geometric growth or geometric decay (the function values form a geometric progression.)

_____ is said to follow an exponential law; the simple-_____ model is known as the Malthusian growth model.

a. Inseparable differential equation
b. Exponential growth
c. Oscillating
d. Isomonodromic deformation

66. In infinitesimal calculus, a _____ is traditionally an infinitesimally small change in a variable. For example, if x is a variable, then a change in the value of x is often denoted Δx (or δx when this change is considered to be small.) The _____ dx represents such a change, but is infinitely small.

a. Differential
b. Related rates
c. Continuous function
d. Dirichlet integral

67. A _____ is a mathematical equation for an unknown function of one or several variables that relates the values of the function itself and of its derivatives of various orders. they play a prominent role in engineering, physics, economics and other disciplines.

A simplified real world example of a _____ is modeling the acceleration of a ball falling through the air (considering only gravity and air resistance.)

a. Lax pair
b. Differential equation
c. Petrovsky lacuna
d. Structural stability

Chapter 3. DIFFERENTIATION RULES

68. The _____ of a quantity whose value decreases with time is the interval required for the quantity to decay to half of its initial value. The concept originated in describing how long it takes atoms to undergo radioactive decay but also applies in a wide variety of other situations.

The term '_____' dates to 1907.

   a. 15 theorem
   c. BIBO stability
   b. BDDC
   d. Half-life

69. _____ is the concept of adding accumulated interest back to the principal, so that interest is earned on interest from that moment on. The act of declaring interest to be principal is called compounding (i.e., interest is compounded.) A loan, for example, may have its interest compounded every month: in this case, a loan with $100 principal and 1% interest per month would have a balance of $101 at the end of the first month.
   a. BIBO stability
   c. 15 theorem
   b. BDDC
   d. Compound interest

70.

In differential calculus, _____ problems involve finding a rate that a quantity changes by relating the population of the earth. The rate of change is usually with respect to people who have died.

   a. Related rates
   c. Binomial series
   b. Complex analysis
   d. Reflection formula

71. In calculus, the _____ is a theorem regarding the limit of a function.

The _____ is a technical result which is very important in proofs in calculus and mathematical analysis. It is typically used to confirm the limit of a function via comparison with two other functions whose limits are known or easily computed.

   a. Squeeze Theorem
   c. Table of limits
   b. Limit of a sequence
   d. 15 theorem

72. In mathematics, a _____ is an approximation of a general function using a linear function (more precisely, an affine function.)

Given a differentiable function f of one real variable, Taylor's theorem for n=1 states that

$$f(x) = f(a) + f\,'(a)(x - a) + R_2$$

where R_2 is the remainder term. The _____ is obtained by dropping the remainder:

$$f(x) \approx f(a) + f\,'(a)(x - a)$$

which is true for x close to a.

    a. Linear approximation
    b. Smooth function
    c. Differentiation of trigonometric functions
    d. Linearity of differentiation

73.   In geometry, the _____ (or simply the tangent) to a curve at a given point is the straight line that 'just touches' the curve at that point (in the sense explained more precisely below.) As it passes through the point of tangency, the _____ is 'going in the same direction' as the curve, and in this sense it is the best straight-line approximation to the curve at that point. The same definition applies to space curves and curves in n-dimensional Euclidean space.
    a. Lie derivative
    b. Sphere
    c. Minimal surface
    d. Tangent line

74.   The _____ in some data is the discrepancy between an exact value and some approximation to it. An _____ can occur because

1. the measurement of the data is not precise (due to the instruments), or
2. approximations are used instead of the real data (e.g., 3.14 instead of π.)

In the mathematical field of numerical analysis, the numerical stability of an algorithm in numerical analysis indicates how the error is propagated by the algorithm.

One commonly distinguishes between the relative error and the absolute error. The absolute error is the magnitude of the difference between the exact value and the approximation.

    a. AUSM
    b. ALGOR
    c. ACTRAN
    d. Approximation error

75.   One commonly distinguishes between the _____ and the absolute error. The absolute error is the magnitude of the difference between the exact value and the approximation. The _____ is the absolute error divided by the magnitude of the exact value.
    a. Series acceleration
    b. Meshfree methods
    c. Numerical integration
    d. Relative error

76.   In calculus, _____ gives a sequence of approximations of a differentiable function around a given point by polynomials (the Taylor polynomials of that function) whose coefficients depend only on the derivatives of the function at that point. The theorem also gives precise estimates on the size of the error in the approximation. The theorem is named after the mathematician Brook Taylor, who stated it in 1712, though the result was first discovered 41 years earlier in 1671 by James Gregory.
    a. Complex analysis
    b. Leibniz differential
    c. Continuous function
    d. Taylor's theorem

77.   In mathematics, the _____ are analogs of the ordinary trigonometric or circular functions. The basic _____ are the hyperbolic sine 'sinh', and the hyperbolic cosine 'cosh', from which are derived the hyperbolic tangent 'tanh', etc., in analogy to the derived trigonometric functions. The inverse _____ are the area hyperbolic sine 'arsinh' (also called 'asinh', or sometimes by the misnomer of 'arcsinh') and so on.

a. Step function
b. Hyperbolic tangent
c. Hyperbolic functions
d. Hyperbolic sine

78. In physics and geometry, the _____ is the theoretical shape of a hanging flexible chain or cable when supported at its ends and acted upon by a uniform gravitational force (its own weight) and in equilibrium. The curve has a U shape that is similar in appearance to the parabola, though it is a different curve.

a. BDDC
b. 15 theorem
c. BIBO stability
d. Catenary

79. In mathematics, the _____ is a conic section, the intersection of a right circular conical surface and a plane parallel to a generating straight line of that surface. Given a point (the focus) and a line (the directrix) that lie in a plane, the locus of points in that plane that are equidistant to them is a _____.

A particular case arises when the plane is tangent to the conical surface of a circle.

a. 15 theorem
b. BDDC
c. BIBO stability
d. Parabola

Chapter 4. APPLICATIONS OF DIFFERENTIATION

1. In a totally ordered set all elements are mutually comparable, so such a set can have at most one minimal element and at most one maximal element. Then, due to mutual comparability, the minimal element will also be the least element and the maximal element will also be the greatest element. Thus in a totally ordered set we can simply use the terms _____ and maximum.

    a. Periodic function
    b. Calculus controversy
    c. Taylor's theorem
    d. Minimum

2. In mathematics, the simplest case of _____ refers to the study of problems in which one seeks to minimize or maximize a real function by systematically choosing the values of real or integer variables from within an allowed set. This (a scalar real valued objective function) is actually a small subset of this field which comprises a large area of applied mathematics and generalizes to study of means to obtain 'best available' values of some objective function given a defined domain where the elaboration is on the types of functions and the conditions and nature of the objects in the problem domain.

The first _____ technique, which is known as steepest descent, goes back to Gauss.

    a. AUSM
    b. ACTRAN
    c. ALGOR
    d. Optimization

3. The largest and the smallest element of a set are called extreme values, absolute extrema, or extreme records.

For a differentiable function f, if $f(x_0)$ is an _____ for the set of all values f(x), and if x_0 is in the interior of the domain of f, then x_0 is a critical point, by Fermat's theorem.

In the case of a general partial order one should not confuse a least element (smaller than all other) and a minimal element (nothing is smaller.)

    a. Integration by substitution
    b. Infinitesimal
    c. Extreme Value Theorem
    d. Extreme Value

4. In calculus, the _____ states that if a real-valued function f is continuous in the closed and bounded interval [a,b], then f must attain its maximum and minimum value, each at least once. That is, there exist numbers c and d in [a,b] such that:

A related theorem is the boundedness theorem which states that a continuous function f in the closed interval [a,b] is bounded on that interval. That is, there exist real numbers m and M such that:

The _____ enriches the boundedness theorem by saying that not only is the function bounded, but it also attains its least upper bound as its maximum and its greatest lower bound as its minimum.

Chapter 4. APPLICATIONS OF DIFFERENTIATION

a. Infinitesimal
c. Integral of secant cubed

b. Uniform convergence
d. Extreme Value Theorem

5. In mathematics, a _____ (or critical number) is a point on the domain of a function where:

   - one dimension: the derivative (or slope of the line when visualized) is equal to zero or a point where the function ceases to be differentiable.
   - in general: there are two distinct concepts: either the derivative (Jacobian) vanishes, or it is not of full rank (or, in either case, the function is not differentiable); these agree in one dimension.

Note that in one dimension, a critical value or critical number x of function f is the domain element at which the derivative is zero or undefined, whereas the associated ordered pair (x, y) is the _____. In higher dimensions a critical value is in the range whereas a _____ is in the domain.

There are two situations in which a point becomes a _____ of a function of one variable. The first of which is that the value of the first derivative is equal to zero.

a. Differential operator
c. Shift theorem

b. Differentiation operator
d. Critical point

6. In mathematics, a _____ is a constant multiplicative factor of a certain object. For example, in the expression $9x^2$, the _____ of x^2 is 9.

The object can be such things as a variable, a vector, a function, etc.

a. Degree of the polynomial
c. Leading coefficient

b. Difference polynomial
d. Coefficient

7. In mathematics, an _____ is an infinite series of the form

$$\sum_{n=0}^{\infty} (-1)^n a_n,$$

with $a_n \geq 0$ (or $a_n \leq 0$) for all n. A finite sum of this kind is an alternating sum. An _____ converges if the terms a_n converge to 0 monotonically.

a. Uniform convergence
c. Extreme value

b. Infinite series
d. Alternating Series

8. In calculus, the _____ is a method of finding the derivative of a function that is the quotient of two other functions for which derivatives exist.

If the function one wishes to differentiate, f(x), can be written as

$$f(x) = \frac{g(x)}{h(x)}$$

and h(x) ≠ 0, then the rule states that the derivative of g(x) / h(x) is equal to:

$$\frac{d}{dx}f(x) = f'(x) = \frac{g'(x)h(x) - g(x)h'(x)}{[h(x)]^2}.$$

Or, more precisely, if all x in some open set containing the number a satisfy h(x) ≠ 0; and g'(a) and h'(a) both exist; then, f'(a) exists as well and:

$$f'(a) = \frac{g'(a)h(a) - g(a)h'(a)}{[h(a)]^2}.$$

The derivative of (4x − 2) / (x² + 1) is:

$$\frac{d}{dx}\left[\frac{(4x-2)}{x^2+1}\right] = \frac{(x^2+1)(4) - (4x-2)(2x)}{(x^2+1)^2}$$
$$= \frac{(4x^2+4) - (8x^2-4x)}{(x^2+1)^2} = \frac{-4x^2+4x+4}{(x^2+1)^2}$$

In the example above, the choices

g(x) = 4x − 2
h(x) = x² + 1

were made. Analogously, the derivative of sin(x) / x² (when x ≠ 0) is:

$$\frac{\cos(x)x^2 - \sin(x)2x}{x^4}$$

Another example is:

$$f(x) = \frac{2x^2}{x^3}$$

whereas g(x) = 2x² and h(x) = x³, and g'(x) = 4x and h'(x) = 3x².

- a. Product rule
- b. Reciprocal Rule
- c. Differentiation rules
- d. Quotient Rule

9. In probability theory and statistics, the _____ (or expectation value or mean and for continuous random variables with a density function it is the probability density -weighted integral of the possible values.

The term '_____' can be misleading.

- a. Expected value
- b. ACTRAN
- c. AUSM
- d. ALGOR

10. In calculus, the _____ states, roughly, that given a section of a smooth curve, there is at least one point on that section at which the derivative (slope) of the curve is equal (parallel) to the 'average' derivative of the section. It is used to prove theorems that make global conclusions about a function on an interval starting from local hypotheses about derivatives at points of the interval.

This theorem can be understood concretely by applying it to motion: If a car travels one hundred miles in one hour, so its average speed during that time was 100 miles per hour.

- a. Mean Value Theorem
- b. Fresnel integrals
- c. First derivative test
- d. Leibniz differential

11. In calculus, a branch of mathematics, the _____ is a measurement of how a function changes when its input changes. Loosely speaking, a _____ can be thought of as how much a quantity is changing at some given point. For example, the _____ of the position (or distance) of a vehicle with respect to time is the instantaneous velocity (respectively, instantaneous speed) at which the vehicle is traveling.

The process of finding a _____ is called differentiation. The fundamental theorem of calculus states that differentiation is the reverse process to integration.

- a. Derivative
- b. Mountain pass theorem
- c. Concave upwards
- d. Ramp function

12. In calculus, the _____ determines whether a given critical point of a function is a maximum, a minimum, or neither.

Suppose that f is a function and we want to determine if f has a maximum or minimum at x. If f is increasing to the left of x and decreasing to the right of x, then x is a local maximum of f.

- a. Hyperbolic angle
- b. Test for Divergence
- c. Functional integration
- d. First Derivative Test

13. In mathematics, an _____ (or purely _____) is a complex number whose squared value is a real number not greater than zero. The imaginary unit, denoted by i or j, is an example of an _____. If y is a real number, then i · y is an _____, because:

$$(i \cdot y)^2 = i^2 \cdot y^2 = -y^2 \leq 0.$$

Imaginary numbers were defined in 1572 by Rafael Bombelli.

    a. Entire function
    b. Edge-of-the-wedge theorem
    c. Univalent function
    d. Imaginary number

14. Cantor defined two kinds of _____ numbers, the ordinal numbers and the cardinal numbers. Ordinal numbers may be identified with well-ordered sets, or counting carried on to any stopping point, including points after an _____ number have already been counted. Generalizing finite and the ordinary _____ sequences which are maps from the positive integers leads to mappings from ordinal numbers, and transfinite sequences.
    a. AUSM
    b. ACTRAN
    c. Infinite
    d. ALGOR

15. In mathematics, a _____ is an ordered list of objects (or events). Like a set, it contains members (also called elements or terms), and the number of terms (possibly infinite) is called the length of the _____. Unlike a set, order matters, and the exact same elements can appear multiple times at different positions in the _____.
    a. Sequence
    b. 15 theorem
    c. BDDC
    d. Y-intercept

16. In differential calculus, an inflection point, or _____ (or inflexion) is a point on a curve at which the curvature changes sign. The curve changes from being concave upwards (positive curvature) to concave downwards (negative curvature), or vice versa. If one imagines driving a vehicle along the curve, it is a point at which the steering-wheel is momentarily 'straight', being turned from left to right or vice versa.
    a. Second derivative test
    b. Point of inflection
    c. Linearity of differentiation
    d. Reduced derivative

17. Let f be a differentiable function, and let f'(x) be its derivative. The derivative of f'(x) (if it has one) is written f''(x) and is called the _____ of f. Similarly, the derivative of a _____, if it exists, is written f'''(x) and is called the third derivative of f.
    a. Stationary phase approximation
    b. Ramp function
    c. Horizontal asymptote
    d. Second Derivative

18. In calculus, a branch of mathematics, the _____ is a criterion often useful for determining whether a given stationary point of a function is a local maximum or a local minimum.

The test states: If the function f is twice differentiable at a stationary point x, meaning that $f'(x) = 0$, then:

- If $f''(x) < 0$ then f has a local maximum at x.
- If $f''(x) > 0$ then f has a local minimum at x.
- If $f''(x) = 0$, the _____ says nothing about the point x, has a possible inflection point.

In the last case, the function may have a local maximum or minimum there, but the function is sufficiently 'flat' that this is undetected by the second derivative. In this case one has to examine the third derivative. Such an example is f(x) = x⁴.

a. Stationary point
c. Metric derivative
b. Parametric derivative
d. Second Derivative Test

19. In calculus and other branches of mathematical analysis, an _____ is an algebraic expression obtained in the context of limits. Limits involving algebraic operations are often performed by replacing subexpressions by their limits; if the expression obtained after this substitution does not give enough information to determine the original limit, it is known as an _____. The indeterminate forms include 0^0, 0/0, 1^∞, ∞ - ∞, ∞/∞, 0×∞, and ∞^0.

a. ACTRAN
c. AUSM
b. ALGOR
d. Indeterminate form

20. In mathematics, the concept of a '_____' is used to describe the behavior of a function as its argument or input either 'gets close' to some point, or as the argument becomes arbitrarily large; or the behavior of a sequence's elements as their index increases indefinitely. Limits are used in calculus and other branches of mathematical analysis to define derivatives and continuity.

In formulas, _____ is usually abbreviated as lim

a. BDDC
c. BIBO stability
b. Limit
d. 15 theorem

21. _____ is the concept of adding accumulated interest back to the principal, so that interest is earned on interest from that moment on. The act of declaring interest to be principal is called compounding (i.e., interest is compounded.) A loan, for example, may have its interest compounded every month: in this case, a loan with $100 principal and 1% interest per month would have a balance of $101 at the end of the first month.

a. 15 theorem
c. BIBO stability
b. Compound interest
d. BDDC

22. Integration is an important concept in mathematics, specifically in the field of calculus and, more broadly, mathematical analysis. Given a function f of a real variable x and an interval [a, b] of the real line, the _____

$$\int_a^b f(x)\, dx,$$

is defined informally to be the net signed area of the region in the xy-plane bounded by the graph of f, the x-axis, and the vertical lines x = a and x = b.

The term '_____' may also refer to the notion of antiderivative, a function F whose derivative is the given function f.

   a. Indefinite integral   b. Integrand
   c. Integral   d. Integral test for convergence

23. An _____ of a real-valued function y = f(x) is a curve which describes the behavior of f as either x or y tends to infinity.

In other words, as one moves along the graph of f(x) in some direction, the distance between it and the _____ eventually becomes smaller than any distance that one may specify.

   a. ALGOR   b. ACTRAN
   c. AUSM   d. Asymptote

24. In mathematics, even functions and odd functions are functions which satisfy particular symmetry relations, with respect to taking additive inverses. They are important in many areas of mathematical analysis, especially the theory of power series and Fourier series. They are named for the parity of the powers of the power functions which satisfy each condition: the function $f(x) = x^n$ is an _____ if n is an even integer, and it is an odd function if n is an odd integer.

   a. Integral of secant cubed   b. Even function
   c. Operational calculus   d. Infinite series

25. Suppose f is a function. Then the line y = a is a _____ for f if

$$\lim_{x \to \infty} f(x) = a \ \text{ or } \ \lim_{x \to -\infty} f(x) = a.$$

Intuitively, this means that f(x) can be made as close as desired to a by making x big enough. How big is big enough depends on how close one wishes to make f(x) to a.

   a. Horizontal asymptote   b. Mountain pass theorem
   c. Bounded function   d. Vertical asymptote

26. In mathematics, even functions and odd functions are functions which satisfy particular symmetry relations, with respect to taking additive inverses. They are important in many areas of mathematical analysis, especially the theory of power series and Fourier series. They are named for the parity of the powers of the power functions which satisfy each condition: the function $f(x) = x^n$ is an even function if n is an even integer, and it is an _____ if n is an odd integer.

   a. Integral of secant cubed   b. Even function
   c. Integration by substitution   d. Odd function

Chapter 4. APPLICATIONS OF DIFFERENTIATION

27. In mathematics, a _____ is a function that repeats its values in regular intervals or periods. The most important examples are the trigonometric functions, which repeat over intervals of length 2π. Periodic functions are used throughout science to describe oscillations, waves, and other phenomena that exhibit periodicity.
    a. Term test
    b. Nth term
    c. Test for Divergence
    d. Periodic function

28. _____ generally conveys two primary meanings. The first is an imprecise sense of harmonious or aesthetically-pleasing proportionality and balance; such that it reflects beauty or perfection. The second meaning is a precise and well-defined concept of balance or 'patterned self-similarity' that can be demonstrated or proved according to the rules of a formal system: by geometry, through physics or otherwise.
    a. 15 theorem
    b. BDDC
    c. BIBO stability
    d. Symmetry

29. The line x = a is a _____ of a curve y=f(x) if at least one of the following statements is true:

    1. $\lim_{x \to a} f(x) = \pm\infty$
    2. $\lim_{x \to a^-} f(x) = \pm\infty$
    3. $\lim_{x \to a^+} f(x) = \pm\infty$

Intuitively, if x = a is an asymptote of f, then, if we imagine x approaching a from one side, the value of f(x) grows without bound; i.e., f(x) becomes large (positively or negatively), and, in fact, becomes larger than any finite value.

Note that f(x) may or may not be defined at a: what the function is doing precisely at x = a does not affect the asymptote. For example, consider the function

$$f(x) = \begin{cases} \frac{1}{x} & \text{if } x > 0, \\ 5 & \text{if } x \leq 0 \end{cases}$$

As $\lim_{x \to 0^+} f(x) = \infty$, f(x) has a _____ at 0, even though f(0) = 5.

Another example is $f(x) = 1/(x-1)$ which has a _____ of x=1 as shown by the limit

$$\lim_{x \to 1^+} \frac{1}{x-1} = \infty$$

In the graph of $f(x) = x + \frac{1}{x}$, the y-axis (x = 0) and the line y = x are both asymptotes.

When a linear asymptote is not parallel to the x- or y-axis, it is called either an oblique asymptote or equivalently a slant asymptote.

a. Vertical asymptote
c. Fractional calculus
b. Geometric function theory
d. Semi-differentiability

30. When a linear asymptote is not parallel to the x- or y-axis, it is called either an oblique asymptote or equivalently a _____. The function f(x) is asymptotic to y = mx + b if

$$\lim_{x \to \infty} f(x) - (mx + b) = 0 \quad \text{or} \quad \lim_{x \to -\infty} f(x) - (mx + b) = 0$$

Note that y = mx + b is never a vertical asymptote, but can be a horizontal asymptote if m=0 (in which case it is not an oblique asymptote.)

An example is $f(x)=(x^2-1)/x$ which has an oblique asymptote of y=x (m=1, b=0) as seen in the limit

$$\lim_{x \to \infty} f(x) - x$$
$$= \lim_{x \to \infty} \frac{x^2 - 1}{x} - x$$
$$= \lim_{x \to \infty} (x - 1/x) - x$$
$$= \lim_{x \to \infty} -1/x = 0$$

Computationally identifying an oblique asymptote can be more difficult than a horizontal or vertical asymptote, in particular because the m and b might not be known.

a. Horizontal asymptote
c. Geometric function theory
b. Slant asymptote
d. Second derivative

31. A _____ or Gompertz function, named after Benjamin Gompertz, is a sigmoid function. It is a type of mathematical model for a time series, where growth is slowest at the start and end of a time period. Graphs of Gompertz curves, showing the effect of varying one of a,b,c while keeping the others constant.

$$y(t) = ae^{be^{ct}}$$

where

- a is the upper asymptote
- c is the growth rate
- b, c are negative numbers
- e is Euler's Number (e = 2.71828...)

Chapter 4. APPLICATIONS OF DIFFERENTIATION

The function curve can be derived from Gompertz's law, which states the rate of mortality (decay) falls exponentially with current size. Mathematically

$$k^r \propto \frac{1}{y(t)}$$

where

- $r = \dfrac{y'(t)}{y(t)}$ is the rate of growth.
- k is an arbitrary constant.

Examples of uses for Gompertz curves include:

- Mobile phone uptake, where costs were initially high (so uptake was slow), followed by a period of rapid growth, followed by a slowing of uptake as saturation was reached.
- Population in a confined space, as birth rates first increase and then slow as resource limits are reached.
- Modeling of growth of tumors

In the sixties A.K. Laird for the first time successfully used the _____ to fit data of growth of tumors. In fact, tumors are cellular populations growing in a confined space where the availability of nutrients is limited.

a. Gompertz curve
b. Duffing equation
c. Neumann-Dirichlet method
d. Spheroidal wave functions

32. In the differential geometry of surfaces, an _____ is a curve always tangent to an asymptotic direction of the surface (where they exist.) It is sometimes called an asymptotic line, although it need not be a line.

An asymptotic direction is one in which the normal curvature is zero.

a. ACTRAN
b. Asymptotic curve
c. Epicycloid
d. ALGOR

33. In mathematics, a (topological) _____ is defined as follows: let I be an interval of real numbers (i.e. a non-empty connected subset of $\mathbb{R}$); then a _____ γ is a continuous mapping $\gamma : I \to X$, where X is a topological space. The _____ γ is said to be simple if it is injective, i.e. if for all x, y in I, we have $\gamma(x) = \gamma(y) \implies x = y$. If I is a closed bounded interval $[a, b]$, we also allow the possibility $\gamma(a) = \gamma(b)$ (this convention makes it possible to talk about closed simple _____.)

a. Prolate cycloid
b. Closed curve
c. Tractrix
d. Curve

34. In calculus, the _____ is a theorem regarding the limit of a function.

Chapter 4. APPLICATIONS OF DIFFERENTIATION

The _____ is a technical result which is very important in proofs in calculus and mathematical analysis. It is typically used to confirm the limit of a function via comparison with two other functions whose limits are known or easily computed.

a. Limit of a sequence
b. 15 theorem
c. Squeeze Theorem
d. Table of limits

35. In mathematics, the _____ is a representation of a function as an infinite sum of terms calculated from the values of its derivatives at a single point. It may be regarded as the limit of the Taylor polynomials. If the series is centered at zero, the series is also called a Maclaurin series.

a. BIBO stability
b. 15 theorem
c. Taylor series
d. BDDC

36. In calculus, the _____ is a formula used to find the derivatives of products of functions. It may be stated thus:

$$(f \cdot g)' = f' \cdot g + f \cdot g'$$

or in the Leibniz notation thus:

$$\frac{d}{dx}(u \cdot v) = u \cdot \frac{dv}{dx} + v \cdot \frac{du}{dx}.$$

Discovery of this rule is credited to Gottfried Leibniz, who demonstrated it using differentials. Here is Leibniz's argument: Let u and v be two differentiable functions of x.

a. Constant factor rule in differentiation
b. Quotient Rule
c. Reciprocal Rule
d. Product Rule

37. In calculus, the _____ is a shorthand method of finding the derivative of a function that is the reciprocal of a differentiable function, without using the quotient rule or chain rule.

The _____ states that the derivative of 1 / g(x) is given by

$$\frac{d}{dx}\left(\frac{1}{g(x)}\right) = \frac{-g'(x)}{(g(x))^2}$$

where $g(x) \neq 0$.

The _____ is derived from the quotient rule, with the numerator f(x) = 1. Then,

It is also possible to derive the _____ from the chain rule, by a process very much like that of the derivation of the quotient rule.

Chapter 4. APPLICATIONS OF DIFFERENTIATION

a. Differentiation rules
c. Constant factor rule in differentiation
b. Reciprocal Rule
d. Quotient Rule

38. In elementary algebra, a _____ is a polynomial with two terms--the sum of two monomials--often bound by parenthesis or brackets when operated upon. It is the simplest kind of polynomial other than monomials.

- The _____ $a^2 - b^2$ can be factored as the product of two other binomials:

    $a^2 - b^2 = (a + b)(a - b.)$

    This is a special case of the more general formula:

    $$a^{n+1} - b^{n+1} = (a - b) \sum_{k=0}^{n} a^k b^{n-k}$$

- The product of a pair of linear binomials (ax + b) and (cx + d) is:

    $(ax + b)(cx + d) = acx^2 + axd + bcx + bd.$

- A _____ raised to the nth power, represented as

    $(a + b)^n$

    can be expanded by means of the _____ theorem or, equivalently, using Pascal's triangle. Taking a simple example, the perfect square _____ $(p + q)^2$ can be found by squaring the :first digit, adding twice the product of the first and second digit and finally adding the square of the second digit, to give $p^2 + 2pq + q^2$.

a. Completing the square
c. Partial fractions
b. Binomial
d. Multinomial theorem

39. In mathematics, the _____ is an important formula giving the expansion of powers of sums. Its simplest version states that

$$(x + y)^n = \sum_{k=0}^{n} \binom{n}{k} x^{n-k} y^k \qquad (1)$$

for any real or complex numbers x and y, and any non-negative integer n. The binomial coefficient appearing in (1) may be defined in terms of the factorial function n!:

$$\binom{n}{k} = \frac{n!}{k!\,(n-k)!}.$$

Chapter 4. APPLICATIONS OF DIFFERENTIATION

For example, here are the cases where 2 ≤ n ≤ 5:

$$(x+y)^2 = x^2 + 2xy + y^2$$
$$(x+y)^3 = x^3 + 3x^2y + 3xy^2 + y^3$$
$$(x+y)^4 = x^4 + 4x^3y + 6x^2y^2 + 4xy^3 + y^4$$
$$(x+y)^5 = x^5 + 5x^4y + 10x^3y^2 + 10x^2y^3 + 5xy^4 + y^5.$$

Formula (1) is valid more generally for any elements x and y of a semiring as long as xy = yx.

- a. Binomial Theorem
- b. Lah numbers
- c. Trinomial expansion
- d. Stirling transform

40. The _____, named after the mathematician Ehrenfried Walther von Tschirnhaus, is a plane curve which is defined by either of these formulae:

$y^2 = x^3 + 3x^2$

$a = r\cos^3(\theta / 3.)$

- a. Kampyle of Eudoxus
- b. Strophoid
- c. Tschirnhausen cubic
- d. Dolbeault operator

41. In calculus, an _____, primitive or indefinite integral of a function f is a function F whose derivative is equal to f, i.e., F >' = f. The process of solving for antiderivatives is antidifferentiation (or indefinite integration.) Antiderivatives are related to definite integrals through the fundamental theorem of calculus: the definite integral of a function over an interval is equal to the difference between the values of an _____ evaluated at the endpoints of the interval.
- a. Integrand
- b. Order of integration
- c. Indefinite integral
- d. Antiderivative

42. The _____ , are the five positions in an orbital configuration where a small object affected only by gravity can theoretically be stationary relative to two larger objects (such as a satellite with respect to the Earth and Moon.) The _____ mark positions where the combined gravitational pull of the two large masses provides precisely the centripetal force required to rotate with them. They are analogous to geostationary orbits in that they allow an object to be in a 'fixed' position in space rather than an orbit in which its relative position changes continuously.
- a. BDDC
- b. 15 theorem
- c. BIBO stability
- d. Lagrangian points

43. In infinitesimal calculus, a _____ is traditionally an infinitesimally small change in a variable. For example, if x is a variable, then a change in the value of x is often denoted Δx (or δx when this change is considered to be small.) The _____ dx represents such a change, but is infinitely small.

Chapter 4. APPLICATIONS OF DIFFERENTIATION

a. Related rates
b. Dirichlet integral
c. Continuous function
d. Differential

44. A _____ is a mathematical equation for an unknown function of one or several variables that relates the values of the function itself and of its derivatives of various orders. they play a prominent role in engineering, physics, economics and other disciplines.

A simplified real world example of a _____ is modeling the acceleration of a ball falling through the air (considering only gravity and air resistance.)

a. Petrovsky lacuna
b. Structural stability
c. Differential equation
d. Lax pair

45. In mathematics and its applications, a _____ system is a system for assigning an n-tuple of numbers or scalars to each point in an n-dimensional space. This concept is part of the theory of manifolds. 'Scalars' in many cases means real numbers, but, depending on context, can mean complex numbers or elements of some other commutative ring.

a. 15 theorem
b. Cylindrical coordinate system
c. Spherical coordinate system
d. Coordinate

46. In mathematics, the _____ is used to determine each point uniquely in a plane through two numbers, usually called the x-coordinate or abscissa and the y-coordinate or ordinate of the point. To define the coordinates, two perpendicular directed lines, are specified, as well as the unit length, which is marked off on the two axes Cartesian coordinate systems are also used in space and in higher dimensions.

a. 15 theorem
b. Cartesian coordinate system
c. Coordinate
d. Spherical coordinate system

Chapter 5. INTEGRALS

1. In mathematics, the _____ is a criterion for the convergence (a convergence test) of an infinite series

$$\sum_{n=1}^{\infty} a_n.$$

It is particularly useful in connection with power series.

The _____ was developed first by Cauchy and so is sometimes known as the Cauchy _____ or Cauchy's radical test.
The _____ uses the number

$$C = \limsup_{n \to \infty} \sqrt[n]{|a_n|},$$

where 'lim sup' denotes the limit superior, possibly ∞.

   a. Related rates
   b. Dirichlet integral
   c. Root Test
   d. Binomial series

2. The _____ is a plane fractal first described by Waclaw Sierpinski in 1916. The carpet is a generalization of the Cantor set to two dimensions (another is Cantor dust.) Sierpinski demonstrated that this fractal is a universal curve, in that any possible one-dimensional graph, projected onto the two-dimensional plane, is homeomorphic to a subset of the _____.
   a. 15 theorem
   b. Siegel disc
   c. BDDC
   d. Sierpinski carpet

3. In mathematics, a (topological) _____ is defined as follows: let I be an interval of real numbers (i.e. a non-empty connected subset of $\mathbb{R}$); then a _____ γ is a continuous mapping $\gamma : I \to X$, where X is a topological space. The _____ γ is said to be simple if it is injective, i.e. if for all x, y in I, we have $\gamma(x) = \gamma(y) \implies x = y$. If I is a closed bounded interval $[a, b]$, we also allow the possibility $\gamma(a) = \gamma(b)$ (this convention makes it possible to talk about closed simple _____.)
   a. Prolate cycloid
   b. Tractrix
   c. Closed curve
   d. Curve

4. _____ is the addition of a set of numbers; the result is their sum or total. An interim or present total of a _____ process is termed the running total. The 'numbers' to be summed may be natural numbers, complex numbers, matrices, or still more complicated objects.
   a. 15 theorem
   b. BDDC
   c. BIBO stability
   d. Summation

5. Integration is an important concept in mathematics, specifically in the field of calculus and, more broadly, mathematical analysis. Given a function f of a real variable x and an interval [a, b] of the real line, the _____

$$\int_a^b f(x)\,dx,$$

is defined informally to be the net signed area of the region in the xy-plane bounded by the graph of f, the x-axis, and the vertical lines x = a and x = b.

The term '_____' may also refer to the notion of antiderivative, a function F whose derivative is the given function f.

    a. Integral test for convergence   b. Integral
    c. Indefinite integral   d. Integrand

6. In mathematics, the concept of a '_____' is used to describe the behavior of a function as its argument or input either 'gets close' to some point, or as the argument becomes arbitrarily large; or the behavior of a sequence's elements as their index increases indefinitely. Limits are used in calculus and other branches of mathematical analysis to define derivatives and continuity.

In formulas, _____ is usually abbreviated as lim

    a. 15 theorem   b. BIBO stability
    c. BDDC   d. Limit

7. If a function has an integral, it is said to be integrable. The function for which the integral is calculated is called the _____. The region over which a function is being integrated is called the domain of integration.
    a. Integration by parts   b. Integral test for convergence
    c. Integrand   d. Order of integration

8. In mathematics, a _____ is an ordered list of objects (or events). Like a set, it contains members (also called elements or terms), and the number of terms (possibly infinite) is called the length of the _____. Unlike a set, order matters, and the exact same elements can appear multiple times at different positions in the _____.
    a. 15 theorem   b. Y-intercept
    c. Sequence   d. BDDC

9. In mathematics, an _____ is an infinite series of the form

$$\sum_{n=0}^{\infty} (-1)^n a_n,$$

with $a_n \geq 0$ (or $a_n \leq 0$) for all n. A finite sum of this kind is an alternating sum. An _____ converges if the terms a_n converge to 0 monotonically.

a. Extreme value
b. Infinite series
c. Uniform convergence
d. Alternating Series

10. In mathematics, a _____ is a function which preserves the given order. This concept first arose in calculus, and was later generalized to the more abstract setting of order theory.

In calculus, a function f defined on a subset of the real numbers with real values is called monotonic (also monotonically increasing or non-decreasing), if for all x and y such that x >≤ y one has f(x) >≤ f(y), so f preserves the order.

a. Pettis integral
b. 15 theorem
c. Pseudo-differential operator
d. Monotonic function

11. In mathematics, a _____ is a method for approximating the total area underneath a curve on a graph, otherwise known as an integral. It may also be used to define the integration operation.

Consider a function $f: D \rightarrow \mathbf{R}$, where D is a subset of the real numbers $\mathbf{R}$, and let $I = [a, b]$ be a closed interval contained in D. A finite set of points $\{x_0, x_1, x_2, \ldots x_n\}$ such that $a = x_0 < x_1 < x_2 \ldots < x_n = b$ creates a partition

$$P = \{[x_0, x_1), [x_1, x_2), \ldots [x_{n-1}, x_n]\}$$

of I.

a. Disk integration
b. Surface of revolution
c. Signed measure
d. Riemann sum

12. The _____ is a function in mathematics. The application of this function to a value x is written as exp(x). Equivalently, this can be written in the form e^x, where e is a mathematical constant, the base of the natural logarithm, which equals approximately 2.718281828, and is also known as Euler's number.

a. Area hyperbolic functions
b. Integral part
c. ACTRAN
d. Exponential function

13. The _____ specifies the relationship between the two central operations of calculus, differentiation and integration.

The first part of the theorem, sometimes called the first _____, shows that an indefinite integration can be reversed by a differentiation.

The second part, sometimes called the second _____, allows one to compute the definite integral of a function by using any one of its infinitely many antiderivatives.

a. Partial sum
b. Calculus controversy
c. Fundamental Theorem of Calculus
d. Minimum

14. In calculus, a branch of mathematics, the _____ is a measurement of how a function changes when its input changes. Loosely speaking, a _____ can be thought of as how much a quantity is changing at some given point. For example, the _____ of the position (or distance) of a vehicle with respect to time is the instantaneous velocity (respectively, instantaneous speed) at which the vehicle is traveling.

The process of finding a _____ is called differentiation. The fundamental theorem of calculus states that differentiation is the reverse process to integration.

- a. Ramp function
- b. Concave upwards
- c. Mountain pass theorem
- d. Derivative

15. In mathematics, the trigonometric integrals are a family of integrals which involve trigonometric functions. A number of the basic trigonometric integrals are discussed at the list of integrals of trigonometric functions. Plot of Si(x) for 0 ≤ x ≤ 8π.

The different _____ definitions are:

$$\text{Si}(x) = \int_0^x \frac{\sin t}{t}\,dt$$

$$\text{si}(x) = -\int_x^\infty \frac{\sin t}{t}\,dt$$

Si(x) is the primitive of sinx / x which is zero for x = 0; si(x) is the primitive of sinx / x which is zero for $x = \infty$.

- a. Trigonometric
- b. Sine integral
- c. 15 theorem
- d. Trigonometric integrals

16. In calculus, an antiderivative, primitive or _____ of a function f is a function F whose derivative is equal to f, i.e., F ′ = f. The process of solving for antiderivatives is antidifferentiation (or indefinite integration.) Antiderivatives are related to definite integrals through the fundamental theorem of calculus: the definite integral of a function over an interval is equal to the difference between the values of an antiderivative evaluated at the endpoints of the interval.

- a. Arc length
- b. Integral test for convergence
- c. Integration by parts operator
- d. Indefinite Integral

17. In mathematics, a _____ is a basic technique used to simplify problems in which the original variables are replaced with new ones; the new and old variables being related in some specified way. The intent is that the problem expressed in new variables may be simpler, or else equivalent to a better understood problem.

A very simple example of a useful variable change can be seen in the problem of finding the roots of the eighth order polynomial:

$$x^8 + 3x^4 + 2 = 0$$

Eighth order polynomial equations are generally impossible to solve in terms of elementary functions.

Chapter 5. INTEGRALS

a. Change of variables
b. BDDC
c. 15 theorem
d. Cubic function

18. In a totally ordered set all elements are mutually comparable, so such a set can have at most one minimal element and at most one maximal element. Then, due to mutual comparability, the minimal element will also be the least element and the maximal element will also be the greatest element. Thus in a totally ordered set we can simply use the terms minimum and _____.

a. Complex analysis
b. Dirichlet integral
c. Hyperbolic angle
d. Maximum

19. In calculus, the _____ is a formula for the derivative of the composite of two functions.

In intuitive terms, if a variable, y, depends on a second variable, u, which in turn depends on a third variable, x, then the rate of change of y with respect to x can be computed as the rate of change of y with respect to u multiplied by the rate of change of u with respect to x. Schematically,

$$\frac{dy}{dx} = \frac{dy}{du} \cdot \frac{du}{dx}.$$

a. Chain Rule
b. Differentiation rules
c. Reciprocal Rule
d. Quotient Rule

20. The _____, named after the mathematician Ehrenfried Walther von Tschirnhaus, is a plane curve which is defined by either of these formulae:

$y^2 = x^3 + 3x^2$

$a = r\cos^3(\theta / 3.)$

a. Strophoid
b. Tschirnhausen cubic
c. Kampyle of Eudoxus
d. Dolbeault operator

21. However, in algebra and in particular in algebraic combinatorics, the term '_____' is often used instead to refer to elements of the ring of symmetric functions, where that ring is a specific limit of the rings of symmetric polynomials in n indeterminates, as n goes to infinity. This ring serves as universal structure in which relations between symmetric polynomials can be expressed in a way independent of the number n of indeterminates (but its elements are neither polynomials nor functions.) Among other things, this ring plays an important role in the representation theory of the symmetric groups.

a. Symmetric function
b. Difference polynomial
c. Leading coefficient
d. Binomial type

22. _____ generally conveys two primary meanings. The first is an imprecise sense of harmonious or aesthetically-pleasing proportionality and balance; such that it reflects beauty or perfection. The second meaning is a precise and well-defined concept of balance or 'patterned self-similarity' that can be demonstrated or proved according to the rules of a formal system: by geometry, through physics or otherwise.
 a. BDDC
 b. 15 theorem
 c. BIBO stability
 d. Symmetry

Chapter 6. APPLICATIONS OF INTEGRATION

1. In calculus, the _____ is a shorthand method of finding the derivative of a function that is the reciprocal of a differentiable function, without using the quotient rule or chain rule.

The _____ states that the derivative of 1 / g(x) is given by

$$\frac{d}{dx}\left(\frac{1}{g(x)}\right) = \frac{-g'(x)}{(g(x))^2}$$

where $g(x) \neq 0$.

The _____ is derived from the quotient rule, with the numerator f(x) = 1. Then,

It is also possible to derive the _____ from the chain rule, by a process very much like that of the derivation of the quotient rule.

- a. Constant factor rule in differentiation
- b. Differentiation rules
- c. Reciprocal Rule
- d. Quotient Rule

2. In mathematics, a (topological) _____ is defined as follows: let I be an interval of real numbers (i.e. a non-empty connected subset of $\mathbb{R}$); then a _____ γ is a continuous mapping $\gamma : I \to X$, where X is a topological space. The _____ γ is said to be simple if it is injective, i.e. if for all x, y in I, we have $\gamma(x) = \gamma(y) \implies x = y$. If I is a closed bounded interval $[a, b]$, we also allow the possibility $\gamma(a) = \gamma(b)$ (this convention makes it possible to talk about closed simple _____.)

- a. Closed curve
- b. Tractrix
- c. Prolate cycloid
- d. Curve

3. The _____, named after the mathematician Ehrenfried Walther von Tschirnhaus, is a plane curve which is defined by either of these formulae:

y² = x³ + 3x²

a = rcos³(θ / 3.)

- a. Strophoid
- b. Dolbeault operator
- c. Tschirnhausen cubic
- d. Kampyle of Eudoxus

4. In a totally ordered set all elements are mutually comparable, so such a set can have at most one minimal element and at most one maximal element. Then, due to mutual comparability, the minimal element will also be the least element and the maximal element will also be the greatest element. Thus in a totally ordered set we can simply use the terms minimum and _____.

- a. Dirichlet integral
- b. Hyperbolic angle
- c. Complex analysis
- d. Maximum

Chapter 6. APPLICATIONS OF INTEGRATION

5. In calculus, the _____ is a formula for the derivative of the composite of two functions.

In intuitive terms, if a variable, y, depends on a second variable, u, which in turn depends on a third variable, x, then the rate of change of y with respect to x can be computed as the rate of change of y with respect to u multiplied by the rate of change of u with respect to x. Schematically,

$$\frac{dy}{dx} = \frac{dy}{du} \cdot \frac{du}{dx}.$$

    a. Reciprocal Rule   b. Quotient Rule
    c. Chain Rule   d. Differentiation rules

6. In mathematics, a _____ is a method for approximating the total area underneath a curve on a graph, otherwise known as an integral. It may also be used to define the integration operation.

Consider a function $f: D \to \mathbf{R}$, where D is a subset of the real numbers $\mathbf{R}$, and let $I = [a, b]$ be a closed interval contained in D. A finite set of points $\{x_0, x_1, x_2, \ldots x_n\}$ such that $a = x_0 < x_1 < x_2 \ldots < x_n = b$ creates a partition

      $P = \{[x_0, x_1), [x_1, x_2), \ldots [x_{n-1}, x_n]\}$

of I.

    a. Signed measure   b. Disk integration
    c. Riemann sum   d. Surface of revolution

7. The _____ is a test to determine if a relation or its graph is a function or not. For a relation or graph to be a function, it can have at most a single y-value for each x-value. Thus, a vertical line drawn at any x-position on the graph of a function will intersect the graph at most once.
    a. 15 theorem   b. BDDC
    c. BIBO stability   d. Vertical Line Test

8. In mathematics, the hyperbolic functions are analogs of the ordinary trigonometric functions. The basic hyperbolic functions are the hyperbolic sine 'sinh', and the _____ 'cosh', from which are derived the hyperbolic tangent 'tanh', etc., in analogy to the derived trigonometric functions. The inverse hyperbolic functions are the area hyperbolic sine 'arsinh' (also called 'asinh', or sometimes by the misnomer of 'arcsinh') and so on.
    a. Heaviside step function   b. Multiplicative inverse
    c. Signum function   d. Hyperbolic cosine

9. In common usage, a cylinder is taken to mean a finite section of a right _____ with its ends closed to form two circular surfaces, as in the figure (right.) If the cylinder has a radius r and length (height) h, then its volume is given by

$$V = \pi r^2 h$$

and its surface area is:

- the area of the top (πr^2) +
- the area of the bottom (πr^2) +
- the area of the side $(2\pi rh)$.

Therefore without the top or bottom (lateral area), the surface area is

$$A = 2\pi rh.$$

With the top and bottom, the surface area is

$$A = 2\pi r^2 + 2\pi rh = 2\pi r(r + h).$$

For a given volume, the cylinder with the smallest surface area has h = 2r. For a given surface area, the cylinder with the largest volume has h = 2r, i.e. the cylinder fits in a cube (height = diameter.)

Cylindric sections are the intersections of cylinders with planes.

   a. Circular cylinder   b. Cylinder
   c. BDDC   d. 15 theorem

10. A _____ is one of the most curvilinear basic geometric shapes: It has two faces, zero vertices, and zero edges. The surface formed by the points at a fixed distance from a given straight line, the axis of the _____. The solid enclosed by this surface and by two planes perpendicular to the axis is also called a _____.
   a. Right circular cylinder   b. BDDC
   c. 15 theorem   d. Cylinder

11. In geometry, a _____ is a three-dimensional figure formed by six parallelograms. It is to a parallelogram as a cube is to a square: Euclidean geometry supports all four notions but affine geometry admits only parallelograms and parallelepipeds. Three equivalent definitions of _____ are

- a polyhedron with six faces (hexahedron), each of which is a parallelogram,
- a hexahedron with three pairs of parallel faces, and
- a prism of which the base is a parallelogram.

The cuboid (six rectangular faces), cube (six square faces), and the rhombohedron (six rhombus faces) are all specific cases of _____.

Parallelepipeds are a subclass of the prismatoids.

a. BDDC
c. BIBO stability

b. 15 theorem
d. Parallelepiped

12. In common usage, a cylinder is taken to mean a finite section of a _____ with its ends closed to form two circular surfaces, as in the figure (right.) If the cylinder has a radius r and length (height) h, then its volume is given by

$$V = \pi r^2 h$$

and its surface area is:

- the area of the top (πr^2) +
- the area of the bottom (πr^2) +
- the area of the side $(2\pi r h)$.

Therefore without the top or bottom (lateral area), the surface area is

$$A = 2\pi r h.$$

With the top and bottom, the surface area is

$$A = 2\pi r^2 + 2\pi r h = 2\pi r (r + h).$$

For a given volume, the cylinder with the smallest surface area has h = 2r. For a given surface area, the cylinder with the largest volume has h = 2r, i.e. the cylinder fits in a cube (height = diameter.)

Cylindric sections are the intersections of cylinders with planes.

a. BDDC
c. Cylinder

b. 15 theorem
d. Right circular cylinder

13. In mathematics, an _____ is an infinite series of the form

$$\sum_{n=0}^{\infty} (-1)^n a_n,$$

with $a_n \geq 0$ (or $a_n \leq 0$) for all n. A finite sum of this kind is an alternating sum. An _____ converges if the terms a_n converge to 0 monotonically.

a. Infinite series
c. Alternating Series

b. Uniform convergence
d. Extreme value

82 *Chapter 6. APPLICATIONS OF INTEGRATION*

14. In mathematics, a _____ is a function which preserves the given order. This concept first arose in calculus, and was later generalized to the more abstract setting of order theory.

In calculus, a function f defined on a subset of the real numbers with real values is called monotonic (also monotonically increasing or non-decreasing), if for all x and y such that x >≤ y one has f(x) >≤ f(y), so f preserves the order.

a. Pettis integral
b. 15 theorem
c. Pseudo-differential operator
d. Monotonic function

15. In mathematics, a _____ is an ordered list of objects (or events). Like a set, it contains members (also called elements or terms), and the number of terms (possibly infinite) is called the length of the _____. Unlike a set, order matters, and the exact same elements can appear multiple times at different positions in the _____.

a. 15 theorem
b. BDDC
c. Sequence
d. Y-intercept

16. In mathematics, the concept of a '_____' is used to describe the behavior of a function as its argument or input either 'gets close' to some point, or as the argument becomes arbitrarily large; or the behavior of a sequence's elements as their index increases indefinitely. Limits are used in calculus and other branches of mathematical analysis to define derivatives and continuity.

In formulas, _____ is usually abbreviated as lim

a. Limit
b. 15 theorem
c. BIBO stability
d. BDDC

17. _____ is a means of calculating the volume of a solid of revolution, when integrating along the axis of revolution. This method models the generated 3 dimensional shape as a 'stack' of an infinite number of disks of infinitesimal thickness. It is possible to use 'washers' instead of 'disks' (the washer method) to obtain 'hollow' solids of revolutions, and uses the same principles that underlie _____.

a. Shell integration
b. Multiple integral
c. Surface of revolution
d. Disk integration

18. In mathematics, engineering, and manufacturing, a _____ is a solid figure obtained by rotating a plane curve around some straight line (the axis) that lies on the same plane.

Assuming that the curve does not cross the axis, the solid's volume is equal to the length of the circle described by the figure's centroid, times the figure's area (Pappus's second centroid Theorem.)

Rotating a curve

A representative disk is a three-dimensional volume element of a _____.

a. Risch algorithm
b. Sum rule in integration
c. Riemann sum
d. Solid of revolution

Chapter 6. APPLICATIONS OF INTEGRATION

19. A _____ is the portion of a solid--normally a cone or pyramid--which lies between two parallel planes cutting the solid. The term is commonly used in computer graphics to describe the 3d area which is visible on the screen (which is formed by a clipped pyramid.)

Each plane section is a base of the _____.

a. BIBO stability
b. Frustum
c. 15 theorem
d. BDDC

20. In geometry, a _____ (pl. tori) is a surface of revolution generated by revolving a circle in three dimensional space about an axis coplanar with the circle, which does not touch the circle. Examples of tori include the surfaces of doughnuts and inner tubes.

a. Torus
b. Prolate
c. Normal vector
d. PDE surfaces

21. In probability theory and statistics, the _____ (or expectation value or mean and for continuous random variables with a density function it is the probability density -weighted integral of the possible values.

The term '_____' can be misleading.

a. Expected value
b. ACTRAN
c. AUSM
d. ALGOR

22. In calculus, the _____ states, roughly, that given a section of a smooth curve, there is at least one point on that section at which the derivative (slope) of the curve is equal (parallel) to the 'average' derivative of the section. It is used to prove theorems that make global conclusions about a function on an interval starting from local hypotheses about derivatives at points of the interval.

This theorem can be understood concretely by applying it to motion: If a car travels one hundred miles in one hour, so its average speed during that time was 100 miles per hour.

a. Leibniz differential
b. First derivative test
c. Fresnel integrals
d. Mean Value Theorem

23. A _____ or Gompertz function, named after Benjamin Gompertz, is a sigmoid function. It is a type of mathematical model for a time series, where growth is slowest at the start and end of a time period. Graphs of Gompertz curves, showing the effect of varying one of a,b,c while keeping the others constant.

$$y(t) = ae^{be^{ct}}$$

where

- a is the upper asymptote
- c is the growth rate
- b, c are negative numbers
- e is Euler's Number (e = 2.71828...)

The function curve can be derived from Gompertz's law, which states the rate of mortality (decay) falls exponentially with current size. Mathematically

$$k^r \propto \frac{1}{y(t)}$$

where

- $r = \dfrac{y'(t)}{y(t)}$ is the rate of growth.
- k is an arbitrary constant.

Examples of uses for Gompertz curves include:

- Mobile phone uptake, where costs were initially high (so uptake was slow), followed by a period of rapid growth, followed by a slowing of uptake as saturation was reached.
- Population in a confined space, as birth rates first increase and then slow as resource limits are reached.
- Modeling of growth of tumors

In the sixties A.K. Laird for the first time successfully used the _____ to fit data of growth of tumors. In fact, tumors are cellular populations growing in a confined space where the availability of nutrients is limited.

a. Duffing equation
c. Neumann-Dirichlet method
b. Spheroidal wave functions
d. Gompertz curve

Chapter 6. APPLICATIONS OF INTEGRATION

24. In mathematical analysis, the _____ states that for each value between the least upper bound and greatest lower bound of the image of a continuous function there is a corresponding value in its domain mapping to the original. _____

- Version I. The _____ states the following: If the function y = f(x) is continuous on the interval [a, b], and u is a number between f(a) and f(b), then there is a c ∈ [a, b] such that f(c) = u.

- Version II. Suppose that I is an interval [a, b] in the real numbers R and that f : I → R is a continuous function. Then the image set f(I) is also an interval, and either it contains [f(a), f(b)], or it contains [f(b), f(a)]; that is,

    f(I) ⊇ [f(a), f(b)], or f(I) ⊇ [f(b), f(a)].

It is frequently stated in the following equivalent form: Suppose that f : [a, b] → R is continuous and that u is a real number satisfying f(a) < u < f(b) or f(a) > u > f(b).) Then for some c ∈ [a, b], f(c) = u.

This captures an intuitive property of continuous functions: given f continuous on [1, 2], if f(1) = 3 and f(2) = 5 then f must take the value 4 somewhere between 1 and 2.

a. AUSM
b. Intermediate Value Theorem
c. ACTRAN
d. ALGOR

25. In physics, and more specifically kinematics, _____ is the change in velocity over time. Because velocity is a vector, it can change in two ways: a change in magnitude and/or a change in direction. In one dimension, _____ is the rate at which something speeds up or slows down.

a. ACTRAN
b. AUSM
c. ALGOR
d. Acceleration

26. The _____ is the derived unit of energy in the International System of Units. It is defined as:

$$1\,\text{J} = 1\,\text{kg} \cdot \text{m}^2 \cdot \text{s}^{-2}$$

One _____ is the amount of energy required to perform the following physical actions:

- The work done by a force of one newton travelling through a distance of one metre;
- The work required to move an electric charge of one coulomb through an electrical potential difference of one volt; or one coulomb volt, with the symbol CÂ·V;
- The work done to produce the power of one watt continuously for one second; or one watt second (compare kilowatt hour), with the symbol WÂ·s. Thus a kilowatt hour is 3,600,000 joules or 3.6 megajoules;

1 _____ is equal to:

- 1×10^7 ergs (exactly)
- 1.6022×10^{19} eV (electronvolts)
- 0.2390 cal (gram calories or small calories)
- 2.3901×10^{-4} kcal (kilocalories, kilogram calories, large calories or food calories)
- 9.4782×10^{-4} BTU (British thermal unit)
- 0.7376 ftÂ·lbf (foot-pound force)
- 23.7 ftÂ·pdl (foot-poundals)
- 2.7778×10^{-7} kilowatt-hour
- 2.7778×10^{-4} watt-hour
- 9.8692×10^{-3} litre-atmosphere
- 1×10^{-44} Foe (exactly)

Units defined in terms of the _____ include:

- 1 thermochemical calorie = 4.184 J
- 1 International Table calorie = 4.1868 J
- 1 watt hour = 3600 J
- 1 kilowatt hour = 3.6×10^6 J (or 3.6 MJ)
- 1 ton TNT exploding = 4.184 GJ

Useful to remember:

- 1 _____ = 1 newton × 1 meter = 1 watt × 1 second

One _____ in everyday life is approximately:

- the energy required to lift a small apple one metre straight up.
- the energy released when that same apple falls one meter to the ground.
- the energy released as heat by a quiet person, every hundredth of a second.
- the energy required to heat one gram of dry, cool air by 1 degree Celsius.
- one hundredth of the energy a person can receive by drinking a drop of beer.
- the kinetic energy of an adult human moving a distance of about a handspan every second.

- Conversion of units
- Orders of magnitude (energy)
- Fluence

a. BDDC
b. BIBO stability
c. Joule
d. 15 theorem

27. The most commonly encountered form of Hooke's law is probably the spring equation, which relates the force exerted by a spring to the distance it is stretched by a _____, k, measured in force per length.

$$F = -kx$$

The negative sign indicates that the force exerted by the spring is in direct opposition to the direction of displacement. It is called a 'restoring force', as it tends to restore the system to equilibrium.

a. Spring constant
b. Navier-Stokes equations
c. 15 theorem
d. Polar moment of inertia

28. The mechanisms of _____; a point mass m_1 attracts another point mass m_2 by a force F_2 which is proportional to the product of the two masses and inversely proportional to the square of the distance (r) between them. Regardless of masses or distance, the magnitudes of $|F_1|$ and $|F_2|$ will always be equal. G is the gravitational constant.

_____ is an empirical physical law describing the gravitational attraction between bodies with mass.

a. 15 theorem
b. Newton's law of universal gravitation
c. BIBO stability
d. BDDC

29. Integration is an important concept in mathematics, specifically in the field of calculus and, more broadly, mathematical analysis. Given a function f of a real variable x and an interval [a, b] of the real line, the _____

$$\int_a^b f(x)\,dx,$$

is defined informally to be the net signed area of the region in the xy-plane bounded by the graph of f, the x-axis, and the vertical lines x = a and x = b.

The term '_____' may also refer to the notion of antiderivative, a function F whose derivative is the given function f.

a. Integrand
b. Indefinite integral
c. Integral test for convergence
d. Integral

Chapter 7. TECHNIQUES OF INTEGRATION

1. In calculus, and more generally in mathematical analysis, _____ is a rule that transforms the integral of products of functions into other, hopefully simpler, integrals. The rule arises from the product rule of differentiation.

If u = f(x), v = g(x), and the differentials du = f '(x) dx and dv = g'(x) dx; then in its simplest form the product rule is:

$$\int u\,dv = uv - \int v\,du.$$

Suppose f(x) and g(x) are two continuously differentiable functions.

   a. Integration by parts
   c. Arc length
   b. Integration by parametric derivatives
   d. Integrand

2. In calculus, the _____ is a shorthand method of finding the derivative of a function that is the reciprocal of a differentiable function, without using the quotient rule or chain rule.

The _____ states that the derivative of 1 / g(x) is given by

$$\frac{d}{dx}\left(\frac{1}{g(x)}\right) = \frac{-g'(x)}{(g(x))^2}$$

where $g(x) \neq 0$.

The _____ is derived from the quotient rule, with the numerator f(x) = 1. Then,

It is also possible to derive the _____ from the chain rule, by a process very much like that of the derivation of the quotient rule.

   a. Differentiation rules
   c. Constant factor rule in differentiation
   b. Quotient Rule
   d. Reciprocal Rule

3. In mathematics, _____ refers to the rewriting of an expression into a simpler form. For example, the process of rewriting a fraction into one with the smallest whole-number denominator possible (while keeping the numerator an integer) is called 'reducing a fraction'. Rewriting a radical (or 'root') expression with the smallest possible whole number under the radical symbol is called 'reducing a radical'.

   a. Reduction
   c. BDDC
   b. BIBO stability
   d. 15 theorem

4. In mathematics, the _____ is a way to approximately calculate the definite integral

$$\int_a^b f(x)\,dx.$$

Chapter 7. TECHNIQUES OF INTEGRATION

The _____ works by approximating the region under the graph of the function f by a trapezoid and calculating its area. It follows that

$$\int_a^b f(x)\,dx \approx (b-a)\frac{f(a)+f(b)}{2}.$$

To calculate this integral more accurately, one first splits the interval of integration [a,b] into n smaller subintervals, and then applies the _____ on each of them. One obtains the composite _____:

$$\int_a^b f(x)\,dx \approx \frac{b-a}{n}\left[\frac{f(a)+f(b)}{2} + \sum_{k=1}^{n-1} f\left(a + k\frac{b-a}{n}\right)\right].$$

This can alternatively be written as:

$$\int_a^b f(x)\,dx \approx \frac{b-a}{2n}\left(f(x_0) + 2f(x_1) + 2f(x_2) + \cdots + 2f(x_{n-1}) + f(x_n)\right)$$

where

$$x_k = a + k\frac{b-a}{n},\ \text{for}\ k = 0, 1, \ldots, n$$

(one can also use a non-uniform grid.)

a. Trapezoidal Rule
b. BDDC
c. 15 theorem
d. BIBO stability

5. Integration is an important concept in mathematics, specifically in the field of calculus and, more broadly, mathematical analysis. Given a function f of a real variable x and an interval [a, b] of the real line, the _____

$$\int_a^b f(x)\,dx,$$

is defined informally to be the net signed area of the region in the xy-plane bounded by the graph of f, the x-axis, and the vertical lines x = a and x = b.

The term '_____' may also refer to the notion of antiderivative, a function F whose derivative is the given function f.

Chapter 7. TECHNIQUES OF INTEGRATION

    a. Indefinite integral
    b. Integrand
    c. Integral test for convergence
    d. Integral

6. Trigonometry is a branch of mathematics that deals with triangles, particularly those plane triangles in which one angle has 90 degrees (right triangles.) Trigonometry deals with relationships between the sides and the angles of triangles and with the _____ functions, which describe those relationships.

Trigonometry has applications in both pure mathematics and in applied mathematics, where it is essential in many branches of science and technology.

    a. Trigonometric integrals
    b. Trigonometric
    c. 15 theorem
    d. Trigonometric functions

7. In mathematics, the _____ are a family of integrals which involve trigonometric functions. A number of the basic _____ are discussed at the list of integrals of trigonometric functions.

The different sine integral definitions are:

$$\mathrm{Si}(x) = \int_0^x \frac{\sin t}{t} dt$$

$$\mathrm{si}(x) = -\int_x^\infty \frac{\sin t}{t} dt$$

Si(x) is the primitive of sinx / x which is zero for x = 0; si(x) is the primitive of sinx / x which is zero for $x = \infty$.

    a. Trigonometric integrals
    b. Trigonometric functions
    c. Trigonometric
    d. 15 theorem

8. In calculus, the _____ is a theorem regarding the limit of a function.

The _____ is a technical result which is very important in proofs in calculus and mathematical analysis. It is typically used to confirm the limit of a function via comparison with two other functions whose limits are known or easily computed.

    a. Limit of a sequence
    b. Squeeze Theorem
    c. 15 theorem
    d. Table of limits

9. In mathematics, a _____ decomposes a periodic function into a sum of simple oscillating functions, namely sines and cosines (or complex exponentials.) The study of _____ is a branch of Fourier analysis. _____ were introduced by Joseph Fourier (1768-1830) for the purpose of solving the heat equation in a metal plate.
    a. BIBO stability
    b. BDDC
    c. 15 theorem
    d. Fourier series

10. In mathematics, _____ is the substitution of trigonometric functions for other expressions. One may use the trigonometric identities to simplify certain integrals containing radical expressions:

- If the integrand contains

$$\sqrt{a^2 - x^2},$$

let

$$x = a \sin \theta$$

and use the identity

$1 - \sin^2\theta = \cos^2\theta$.

- If the integrand contains

$$\sqrt{a^2 + x^2}$$

let $x = a \tan \theta$
and use the identity

$$1 + \tan^2 \theta = \sec^2 \theta.$$

- If the integrand contains

$$\sqrt{x^2 - a^2}$$

let

$$x = a \sec \theta$$

and use the identity

$$\sec^2 \theta - 1 = \tan^2 \theta.$$

In the integral

$$\int \frac{dx}{\sqrt{a^2 - x^2}}$$

we may use

$$x = a\sin(\theta), \ dx = a\cos(\theta)\, d\theta$$
$$\theta = \arcsin\left(\frac{x}{a}\right)$$

so that the integral becomes

$$\int \frac{dx}{\sqrt{a^2 - x^2}} = \int \frac{a\cos(\theta)\, d\theta}{\sqrt{a^2 - a^2\sin^2(\theta)}} = \int \frac{a\cos(\theta)\, d\theta}{\sqrt{a^2(1 - \sin^2(\theta))}}$$
$$= \int \frac{a\cos(\theta)\, d\theta}{\sqrt{a^2\cos^2(\theta)}} = \int d\theta = \theta + C = \arcsin\left(\frac{x}{a}\right) + C$$

Note that the above step requires that a > 0 and cos(θ) > 0; we can choose the a to be the positive square root of a²; and we impose the restriction on θ to be −π/2 < θ < π/2 by using the arcsin function.

For a definite integral, one must figure out how the bounds of integration change. For example, as x goes from 0 to a/2, then sin (θ) goes from 0 to 1/2, so θ goes from 0 to π/6.

    a. Signed measure   b. Trigonometric substitution
    c. Surface of revolution   d. Linearity of integration

11. In mathematics, an _____, is the apparent shape of a circle viewed obliquely from outside it, as distinct from a hyperbola which is the shape seen from inside. It is the finite or bounded case of a conic section as a shape cut in a cone by a plane, the unbounded cases being the parabola, which like the _____ remains connected, and the hyperbola, which separates into two connected components or branches.

Equivalently an _____ can be defined as the locus of points, or path traced out, in a plane such that the sum of the distances from the moving point to two fixed points remains constant.

    a. ACTRAN   b. ALGOR
    c. AUSM   d. Ellipse

12. In a totally ordered set all elements are mutually comparable, so such a set can have at most one minimal element and at most one maximal element. Then, due to mutual comparability, the minimal element will also be the least element and the maximal element will also be the greatest element. Thus in a totally ordered set we can simply use the terms minimum and _____.

    a. Dirichlet integral   b. Complex analysis
    c. Hyperbolic angle   d. Maximum

13. In calculus, the _____ is a formula for the derivative of the composite of two functions.

Chapter 7. TECHNIQUES OF INTEGRATION

In intuitive terms, if a variable, y, depends on a second variable, u, which in turn depends on a third variable, x, then the rate of change of y with respect to x can be computed as the rate of change of y with respect to u multiplied by the rate of change of u with respect to x. Schematically,

$$\frac{dy}{dx} = \frac{dy}{du} \cdot \frac{du}{dx}.$$

a. Chain Rule
c. Quotient Rule

b. Reciprocal Rule
d. Differentiation rules

14. In calculus, the _____ is a method of finding the derivative of a function that is the quotient of two other functions for which derivatives exist.

If the function one wishes to differentiate, f(x), can be written as

$$f(x) = \frac{g(x)}{h(x)}$$

and h(x) ≠ 0, then the rule states that the derivative of g(x) / h(x) is equal to:

$$\frac{d}{dx}f(x) = f'(x) = \frac{g'(x)h(x) - g(x)h'(x)}{[h(x)]^2}.$$

Or, more precisely, if all x in some open set containing the number a satisfy h(x) ≠ 0; and g'(a) and h'(a) both exist; then, f'(a) exists as well and:

$$f'(a) = \frac{g'(a)h(a) - g(a)h'(a)}{[h(a)]^2}.$$

The derivative of (4x − 2) / (x² + 1) is:

$$\frac{d}{dx}\left[\frac{(4x-2)}{x^2+1}\right] = \frac{(x^2+1)(4) - (4x-2)(2x)}{(x^2+1)^2}$$

$$= \frac{(4x^2+4) - (8x^2-4x)}{(x^2+1)^2} \qquad = \frac{-4x^2+4x+4}{(x^2+1)^2}$$

Chapter 7. TECHNIQUES OF INTEGRATION

In the example above, the choices

g(x) = 4x − 2
h(x) = x² + 1

were made. Analogously, the derivative of sin(x) / x² (when x ≠ 0) is:

$$\frac{\cos(x)x^2 - \sin(x)2x}{x^4}$$

Another example is:

$$f(x) = \frac{2x^2}{x^3}$$

whereas g(x) = 2x² and h(x) = x³, and g'(x) = 4x and h'(x) = 3x².

a. Reciprocal Rule
c. Product rule
b. Quotient Rule
d. Differentiation rules

15. In integral calculus we would want to write a fractional algebraic expression as the sum of its _____ in order to take the integral of each simple fraction separately. Once the original denominator, D_0, has been factored we set up a fraction for each factor in the denominator. We may use a subscripted D to represent the denominator of the respective _____ which are the factors in D_0.

a. Completing the square
c. Hurwitz quaternion order
b. Multinomial theorem
d. Partial fractions

16. In mathematics, an _____ is a function built from a finite number of exponentials, logarithms, constants, one variable, and nth roots through composition and combinations using the four elementary operations (+ - × ÷.) The trigonometric functions and their inverses are assumed to be included in the elementary functions by using complex variables and the relations between the trigonometric functions and the exponential and logarithm functions.

Elementary functions are considered a subset of special functions.

a. AUSM
c. ALGOR
b. ACTRAN
d. Elementary function

17. In mathematics, an _____ is an infinite series of the form

$$\sum_{n=0}^{\infty}(-1)^n a_n,$$

with $a_n \geq 0$ (or $a_n \leq 0$) for all n. A finite sum of this kind is an alternating sum. An _____ converges if the terms a_n converge to 0 monotonically.

a. Extreme value
b. Uniform convergence
c. Infinite series
d. Alternating Series

18. In numerical analysis, _____ constitutes a broad family of algorithms for calculating the numerical value of a definite integral, and by extension, the term is also sometimes used to describe the numerical solution of differential equations The term numerical quadrature is more or less a synonym for _____, especially as applied to one-dimensional integrals.

a. Meshfree methods
b. Numerical integration
c. Galerkin methods
d. Multigrid method

19. The _____ are a pair of first order, non-linear, differential equations frequently used to describe the dynamics of biological systems in which two species interact, one a predator and one its prey. They were proposed independently by Alfred J. Lotka in 1925 and Vito Volterra in 1926.

where

- y is the number of some predator;
- x is the number of its prey;
- dy/dt and dx/dt represents the growth of the two populations against time;
- t represents the time; and
- >α, >β, >γ and >δ are parameters representing the interaction of the two species.

When multiplied out, the equations take a form useful for physical interpretation. Their origin should be considered from a more general framework,

where both functions represent per capita growth rates of the prey and predator, respectively.

a. BDDC
b. BIBO stability
c. 15 theorem
d. Lotka-Volterra equations

20. In calculus, an _____ is the limit of a definite integral as an endpoint of the interval of integration approaches either a specified real number or ∞ or −∞ or, in some cases, as both endpoints approach limits.

Specifically, an _____ is a limit of the form

$$\lim_{b \to \infty} \int_a^b f(x)\,dx, \qquad \lim_{a \to -\infty} \int_a^b f(x)\,dx,$$

or of the form

$$\lim_{c \to b^-} \int_a^c f(x)\,dx, \qquad \lim_{c \to a^+} \int_c^b f(x)\,dx,$$

in which one takes a limit in one or the other (or sometimes both) endpoints. Improper integrals may also occur at an interior point of the domain of integration, or at multiple such points.

    a. AUSM   b. ACTRAN
    c. ALGOR   d. Improper integral

21. Cantor defined two kinds of _____ numbers, the ordinal numbers and the cardinal numbers. Ordinal numbers may be identified with well-ordered sets, or counting carried on to any stopping point, including points after an _____ number have already been counted. Generalizing finite and the ordinary _____ sequences which are maps from the positive integers leads to mappings from ordinal numbers, and transfinite sequences.

    a. ALGOR   b. AUSM
    c. ACTRAN   d. Infinite

22. In probability theory, a probability distribution is called continuous if its cumulative distribution function is continuous. This is equivalent to saying that for random variables X with the distribution in question, Pr[X = a] = 0 for all real numbers a, i.e.: the probability that X attains the value a is zero, for any number a. If the distribution of X is continuous then X is called a _____.

    a. Linear regression   b. Continuous random variable
    c. Standard deviation   d. Moment

23. In vector calculus, the _____ is an operator that measures the magnitude of a vector field's source or sink at a given point; the _____ of a vector field is a (signed) scalar. For example, consider air as it is heated or cooled. The relevant vector field for this example is the velocity of the moving air at a point.

    a. Divergence Theorem   b. Triple product
    c. Gradient theorem   d. Divergence

24. If a function has an integral, it is said to be integrable. The function for which the integral is calculated is called the _____. The region over which a function is being integrated is called the domain of integration.

    a. Integral test for convergence   b. Order of integration
    c. Integrand   d. Integration by parts

Chapter 7. TECHNIQUES OF INTEGRATION

25. In mathematics, the _____ is a representation of a function as an infinite sum of terms calculated from the values of its derivatives at a single point. It may be regarded as the limit of the Taylor polynomials. If the series is centered at zero, the series is also called a Maclaurin series.
    a. BIBO stability
    b. 15 theorem
    c. BDDC
    d. Taylor series

26. In probability theory and statistics, the _____ (or expectation value or mean and for continuous random variables with a density function it is the probability density -weighted integral of the possible values.

    The term '_____' can be misleading.

    a. ALGOR
    b. Expected value
    c. ACTRAN
    d. AUSM

27. In physics, _____ is defined as the rate of change of position. it is vector physical quantity; both speed and direction are required to define it. In the SI (metric) system, it is measured in meters per second: (m/s) or ms^{-1}.
    a. BDDC
    b. BIBO stability
    c. 15 theorem
    d. Velocity

Chapter 8. FURTHER APPLICATIONS OF INTEGRATION

1. In calculus, _____, was originally the use of expressions such as dx and dy and to represent 'infinitely small' (or infinitesimal) increments of quantities x and y, just as >Δx and >Δy represent finite increments of x and y respectively. So for y being a function of x, or

the derivative of y with respect to x, which later came to be viewed as

was, according to Leibniz, the quotient of an infinitesimal increment of y by an infinitesimal increment of x, or

where the right hand side is Lagrange's notation for the derivative of f at x.

Similarly, although mathematicians usually now view an integral

as a limit

where >Δx is an interval containing x_i, Leibniz viewed it as the sum (the integral sign denoting summation) of infinitely many infinitesimal quantities f(x) dx.

a. Fermat differentiation
b. Leibniz's notation
c. Notation for differentiation
d. Gradient

2. For some curves there is a smallest number L that is an upper bound on the length of any polygonal approximation. If such a number exists, then the curve is said to be rectifiable and the curve is defined to have _____ L.

Let C be a curve in Euclidean (or, generally, a metric) space X = R^n, so C is the image of a continuous function f : [a, b] → X of the interval [a, b] into X.

a. Arc length
b. Integrand
c. Order of integration
d. Integration by parametric derivatives

Chapter 8. FURTHER APPLICATIONS OF INTEGRATION

3. In mathematics, a (topological) _____ is defined as follows: let I be an interval of real numbers (i.e. a non-empty connected subset of $\mathbb{R}$); then a _____ γ is a continuous mapping $\gamma : I \to X$, where X is a topological space. The _____ γ is said to be simple if it is injective, i.e. if for all x, y in I, we have $\gamma(x) = \gamma(y) \implies x = y$. If I is a closed bounded interval $[a, b]$, we also allow the possibility $\gamma(a) = \gamma(b)$ (this convention makes it possible to talk about closed simple _____.)

   a. Prolate cycloid   b. Closed curve
   c. Tractrix   d. Curve

4. Determining the _____ segment -- also called rectification of a curve -- was historically difficult. Although many methods were used for specific curves, the advent of calculus led to a general formula that provides closed-form solutions in some cases.

A curve in, say, the plane can be approximated by connecting a finite number of points on the curve using line segments to create a polygonal path. Since it is straightforward to calculate the length of each linear segment (using the theorem of Pythagoras in Euclidean space, for example), the total length of the approximation can be found by summing the lengths of each linear segment.

   a. Surface of revolution   b. Riemann sum
   c. Nonelementary integral   d. Length of an irregular arc

5. Smooth functions with given closed support are used in the construction of smooth partitions of unity ; these are essential in the study of smooth manifolds, for example to show that Riemannian metrics can be defined globally starting from their local existence. A simple case is that of a bump function on the real line, that is, a _____ f that takes the value 0 outside an interval [a,b] and such that

        f(x) > 0 for a < x < b.

Given a number of overlapping intervals on the line, bump functions can be constructed on each of them, and on semi-infinite intervals (->∞, c] and [d,+>∞) to cover the whole line, such that the sum of the functions is always 1.

   a. Linear approximation   b. Smooth function
   c. Symmetrically continuous   d. Functional derivative

6. The largest and the smallest element of a set are called extreme values, absolute extrema, or extreme records.

For a differentiable function f, if $f(x_0)$ is an _____ for the set of all values f(x), and if x_0 is in the interior of the domain of f, then x_0 is a critical point, by Fermat's theorem.

In the case of a general partial order one should not confuse a least element (smaller than all other) and a minimal element (nothing is smaller.)

   a. Integration by substitution   b. Infinitesimal
   c. Extreme Value Theorem   d. Extreme Value

7. In calculus, the _____ states that if a real-valued function f is continuous in the closed and bounded interval [a,b], then f must attain its maximum and minimum value, each at least once. That is, there exist numbers c and d in [a,b] such that:

A related theorem is the boundedness theorem which states that a continuous function f in the closed interval [a,b] is bounded on that interval. That is, there exist real numbers m and M such that:

The _____ enriches the boundedness theorem by saying that not only is the function bounded, but it also attains its least upper bound as its maximum and its greatest lower bound as its minimum.

   a. Uniform convergence
   c. Integral of secant cubed
   b. Extreme Value Theorem
   d. Infinitesimal

8. In calculus, the _____ is a shorthand method of finding the derivative of a function that is the reciprocal of a differentiable function, without using the quotient rule or chain rule.

The _____ states that the derivative of 1 / g(x) is given by

$$\frac{d}{dx}\left(\frac{1}{g(x)}\right) = \frac{-g'(x)}{(g(x))^2}$$

where $g(x) \neq 0$.

The _____ is derived from the quotient rule, with the numerator f(x) = 1. Then,

   It is also possible to derive the _____ from the chain rule, by a process very much like that of the derivation of the quotient rule.

   a. Differentiation rules
   c. Constant factor rule in differentiation
   b. Quotient Rule
   d. Reciprocal Rule

9. A _____ is a surface created by rotating a curve lying on some plane (the generatrix) around a straight line (the axis of rotation) that lies on the same plane.

Examples of surfaces generated by a straight line are the cylindrical and conical surfaces. A circle that is rotated about a (coplanar) axis through the center generates a sphere.

a. Solid of revolution
c. Disk integration

b. Nonelementary integral
d. Surface of revolution

10. In mathematics, an _____ is an infinite series of the form

$$\sum_{n=0}^{\infty}(-1)^n a_n,$$

with $a_n \geq 0$ (or $a_n \leq 0$) for all n. A finite sum of this kind is an alternating sum. An _____ converges if the terms a_n converge to 0 monotonically.

a. Uniform convergence
c. Extreme value

b. Infinite series
d. Alternating Series

11. _____ is how much exposed area an object has. It is expressed in square units. If an object has flat faces, its _____ can be calculated by adding together the areas of its faces.
a. Plane curve
c. Lipschitz domain

b. Surface area
d. Gyroid

12. The _____ is a test to determine if a relation or its graph is a function or not. For a relation or graph to be a function, it can have at most a single y-value for each x-value. Thus, a vertical line drawn at any x-position on the graph of a function will intersect the graph at most once.
a. BDDC
c. Vertical Line Test

b. BIBO stability
d. 15 theorem

13. In mathematics, engineering, and manufacturing, a _____ is a solid figure obtained by rotating a plane curve around some straight line (the axis) that lies on the same plane.

Assuming that the curve does not cross the axis, the solid's volume is equal to the length of the circle described by the figure's centroid, times the figure's area (Pappus's second centroid Theorem.)

Rotating a curve

A representative disk is a three-dimensional volume element of a _____.

a. Riemann sum
c. Risch algorithm

b. Sum rule in integration
d. Solid of revolution

14. In mathematics, the concept of a '_____' is used to describe the behavior of a function as its argument or input either 'gets close' to some point, or as the argument becomes arbitrarily large; or the behavior of a sequence's elements as their index increases indefinitely. Limits are used in calculus and other branches of mathematical analysis to define derivatives and continuity.

In formulas, _____ is usually abbreviated as lim

a. Limit
b. 15 theorem
c. BIBO stability
d. BDDC

15. This article will state and prove the _____ for differentiation, and then use it to prove these two formulas.

The _____ for differentiation states that for every natural number n, the derivative of $f(x) = x^n$ is $f'(x) = nx^{n-1}$, that is,

$$(x^n)' = nx^{n-1}.$$

The _____ for integration

$$\int x^n \, dx = \frac{x^{n+1}}{n+1} + C$$

for natural n is then an easy consequence. One just needs to take the derivative of this equality and use the _____ and linearity of differentiation on the right-hand side.

a. Limits of integration
b. Hyperbolic angle
c. Dirichlet integral
d. Power Rule

16. In mathematics, a _____ is an ordered list of objects (or events). Like a set, it contains members (also called elements or terms), and the number of terms (possibly infinite) is called the length of the _____. Unlike a set, order matters, and the exact same elements can appear multiple times at different positions in the _____.
a. Sequence
b. Y-intercept
c. BDDC
d. 15 theorem

17. In mathematics, the _____ is a representation of a function as an infinite sum of terms calculated from the values of its derivatives at a single point. It may be regarded as the limit of the Taylor polynomials. If the series is centered at zero, the series is also called a Maclaurin series.
a. BDDC
b. BIBO stability
c. Taylor series
d. 15 theorem

18. A _____ or Gompertz function, named after Benjamin Gompertz, is a sigmoid function. It is a type of mathematical model for a time series, where growth is slowest at the start and end of a time period. Graphs of Gompertz curves, showing the effect of varying one of a,b,c while keeping the others constant.

$$y(t) = ae^{be^{ct}}$$

where

- a is the upper asymptote
- c is the growth rate
- b, c are negative numbers
- e is Euler's Number (e = 2.71828...)

The function curve can be derived from Gompertz's law, which states the rate of mortality (decay) falls exponentially with current size. Mathematically

$$k^r \propto \frac{1}{y(t)}$$

where

- $r = \dfrac{y'(t)}{y(t)}$ is the rate of growth.
- k is an arbitrary constant.

Examples of uses for Gompertz curves include:

- Mobile phone uptake, where costs were initially high (so uptake was slow), followed by a period of rapid growth, followed by a slowing of uptake as saturation was reached.
- Population in a confined space, as birth rates first increase and then slow as resource limits are reached.
- Modeling of growth of tumors

In the sixties A.K. Laird for the first time successfully used the _____ to fit data of growth of tumors. In fact, tumors are cellular populations growing in a confined space where the availability of nutrients is limited.

a. Duffing equation
b. Spheroidal wave functions
c. Neumann-Dirichlet method
d. Gompertz curve

19. The concept of _____ in mathematics evolved from the concept of _____ in physics. The nth _____ of a real-valued function f(x) of a real variable about a value c is

$$\mu'_n = \int_{-\infty}^{\infty} (x-c)^n f(x)\, dx.$$

It is possible to define moments for random variables in a more general fashion than moments for real values. See Moments in metric spaces.

Chapter 8. FURTHER APPLICATIONS OF INTEGRATION

a. Linear regression
c. Poisson distribution
b. Moment
d. Standard deviation

20. _____ generally conveys two primary meanings. The first is an imprecise sense of harmonious or aesthetically-pleasing proportionality and balance; such that it reflects beauty or perfection. The second meaning is a precise and well-defined concept of balance or 'patterned self-similarity' that can be demonstrated or proved according to the rules of a formal system: by geometry, through physics or otherwise.

a. BIBO stability
c. BDDC
b. Symmetry
d. 15 theorem

21. In calculus, the _____ allows you to take constants outside a derivative and concentrate on differentiating the function of x itself. This is a part of the linearity of differentiation.

Suppose you have a function

$$g(x) = k \cdot f(x).$$

where k is a constant.

Use the formula for differentiation from first principles to obtain:

$$g'(x) = \lim_{h \to 0} \frac{g(x+h) - g(x)}{h}$$
$$g'(x) = \lim_{h \to 0} \frac{k \cdot f(x+h) - k \cdot f(x)}{h}$$
$$g'(x) = \lim_{h \to 0} \frac{k(f(x+h) - f(x))}{h}$$
$$g'(x) = k \lim_{h \to 0} \frac{f(x+h) - f(x)}{h} \quad (*)$$
$$g'(x) = k \cdot f'(x).$$

This is the statement of the _____, in Lagrange's notation for differentiation.

a. Product rule
c. Reciprocal Rule
b. Differentiation rules
d. Constant factor rule in differentiation

22. In elementary algebra, a _____ is a polynomial with two terms--the sum of two monomials--often bound by parenthesis or brackets when operated upon. It is the simplest kind of polynomial other than monomials.

- The _____ $a^2 - b^2$ can be factored as the product of two other binomials:

    $a^2 - b^2 = (a + b)(a - b.)$

    This is a special case of the more general formula:

    $$a^{n+1} - b^{n+1} = (a - b) \sum_{k=0}^{n} a^k b^{n-k}.$$

- The product of a pair of linear binomials (ax + b) and (cx + d) is:

    $(ax + b)(cx + d) = acx^2 + axd + bcx + bd.$

- A _____ raised to the nth power, represented as

    $(a + b)^n$

    can be expanded by means of the _____ theorem or, equivalently, using Pascal's triangle. Taking a simple example, the perfect square _____ $(p + q)^2$ can be found by squaring the first digit, adding twice the product of the first and second digit and finally adding the square of the second digit, to give $p^2 + 2pq + q^2$.

a. Multinomial theorem
b. Partial fractions
c. Completing the square
d. Binomial

23. In mathematics, the _____ is an important formula giving the expansion of powers of sums. Its simplest version states that

$$(x + y)^n = \sum_{k=0}^{n} \binom{n}{k} x^{n-k} y^k \qquad (1)$$

for any real or complex numbers x and y, and any non-negative integer n. The binomial coefficient appearing in (1) may be defined in terms of the factorial function n!:

$$\binom{n}{k} = \frac{n!}{k!\,(n-k)!}.$$

For example, here are the cases where 2 ≤ n ≤ 5:

$$(x+y)^2 = x^2 + 2xy + y^2$$
$$(x+y)^3 = x^3 + 3x^2y + 3xy^2 + y^3$$
$$(x+y)^4 = x^4 + 4x^3y + 6x^2y^2 + 4xy^3 + y^4$$
$$(x+y)^5 = x^5 + 5x^4y + 10x^3y^2 + 10x^2y^3 + 5xy^4 + y^5.$$

Formula (1) is valid more generally for any elements x and y of a semiring as long as xy = yx.

- a. Lah numbers
- b. Trinomial expansion
- c. Stirling transform
- d. Binomial Theorem

24. In calculus, a branch of mathematics, the _____ is a measurement of how a function changes when its input changes. Loosely speaking, a _____ can be thought of as how much a quantity is changing at some given point. For example, the _____ of the position (or distance) of a vehicle with respect to time is the instantaneous velocity (respectively, instantaneous speed) at which the vehicle is traveling.

The process of finding a _____ is called differentiation. The fundamental theorem of calculus states that differentiation is the reverse process to integration.

- a. Derivative
- b. Concave upwards
- c. Ramp function
- d. Mountain pass theorem

25. In calculus, the _____ determines whether a given critical point of a function is a maximum, a minimum, or neither.

Suppose that f is a function and we want to determine if f has a maximum or minimum at x. If f is increasing to the left of x and decreasing to the right of x, then x is a local maximum of f.

- a. Functional integration
- b. Test for Divergence
- c. First Derivative Test
- d. Hyperbolic angle

Chapter 8. FURTHER APPLICATIONS OF INTEGRATION

26. In the various subfields of physics, there exist two common usages of the term _____, both with rigorous mathematical frameworks.

- In the study of transport phenomena (heat transfer, mass transfer and fluid dynamics), _____ is defined as the amount that flows through a unit area per unit time. _____ in this definition is a vector.
- In the field of electromagnetism and mathematics, _____ is usually the integral of a vector quantity over a finite surface. The result of this integration is a scalar quantity. The magnetic _____ is thus the integral of the magnetic vector field B over a surface, and the electric _____ is defined similarly. Using this definition, the _____ of the Poynting vector over a specified surface is the rate at which electromagnetic energy flows through that surface. Confusingly, the Poynting vector is sometimes called the power _____, which is an example of the first usage of _____, above. It has units of watts per square metre (WÂ·m^{-2})

One could argue, based on the work of James Clerk Maxwell, that the transport definition precedes the more recent way the term is used in electromagnetism. The specific quote from Maxwell is 'In the case of fluxes, we have to take the integral, over a surface, of the _____ through every element of the surface. The result of this operation is called the surface integral of the _____.

 a. BIBO stability
 b. BDDC
 c. 15 theorem
 d. Flux

27. In mathematics, the _____, introduced by German mathematician Georg Cantor in 1883 (but discovered in 1875 by Henry John Stephen Smith), is a set of points lying on a single line segment that has a number of remarkable and deep properties. Through consideration of it, Cantor and others helped lay the foundations of modern general topology. Although Cantor himself defined the set in a general, abstract way, the most common modern construction is the Cantor ternary set, built by removing the middle thirds of a line segment.
 a. Planar Lamina
 b. BDDC
 c. Cantor set
 d. 15 theorem

28. In probability theory, a probability distribution is called continuous if its cumulative distribution function is continuous. This is equivalent to saying that for random variables X with the distribution in question, Pr[X = a] = 0 for all real numbers a, i.e.: the probability that X attains the value a is zero, for any number a. If the distribution of X is continuous then X is called a _____.
 a. Linear regression
 b. Moment
 c. Continuous random variable
 d. Standard deviation

29. The _____ of a material is defined as its mass per unit volume. The symbol of _____ is ρ '>rho.)

Mathematically:

$$d = \frac{m}{V}$$

where:

        d is the _____,
        m is the mass,
        V is the volume.

a. BDDC
b. BIBO stability
c. 15 theorem
d. Density

30. In mathematics, a _____ (pdf) is a function that represents a probability distribution in terms of integrals.

Formally, a probability distribution has density f, if f is a non-negative Lebesgue-integrable function $\mathbb{R} \to \mathbb{R}$ such that the probability of the interval [a, b] is given by

$$\int_a^b f(x)\, dx$$

for any two numbers a and b. This implies that the total integral of f must be 1.

a. BIBO stability
b. Probability density function
c. 15 theorem
d. BDDC

31. In probability theory and statistics, the _____ (or expectation value or mean and for continuous random variables with a density function it is the probability density -weighted integral of the possible values.

The term '_____' can be misleading.

a. ACTRAN
b. ALGOR
c. AUSM
d. Expected value

32. In calculus, the _____ states, roughly, that given a section of a smooth curve, there is at least one point on that section at which the derivative (slope) of the curve is equal (parallel) to the 'average' derivative of the section. It is used to prove theorems that make global conclusions about a function on an interval starting from local hypotheses about derivatives at points of the interval.

This theorem can be understood concretely by applying it to motion: If a car travels one hundred miles in one hour, so its average speed during that time was 100 miles per hour.

a. Mean Value Theorem
b. First derivative test
c. Leibniz differential
d. Fresnel integrals

33. In calculus, the _____ is a theorem regarding the limit of a function.

The _____ is a technical result which is very important in proofs in calculus and mathematical analysis. It is typically used to confirm the limit of a function via comparison with two other functions whose limits are known or easily computed.

   a. 15 theorem
   c. Squeeze Theorem
   b. Limit of a sequence
   d. Table of limits

34. The _____ is an important family of continuous probability distributions, applicable in many fields. Each member of the family may be defined by two parameters, location and scale: the mean and variance respectively. The standard _____ is the _____ with a mean of zero and a variance of one.
   a. Linear regression
   c. Continuous random variable
   b. Poisson distribution
   d. Normal distribution

35. In statistics, _____ is a simple measure of the variability or dispersion of a data set. A low _____ indicates that all of the data points are very close to the same value (the mean), while high _____ indicates that the data is 'spread out' over a large range of values.

For example, the average height for adult men in the United States is about 70 inches, with a _____ of around 3 inches.

   a. Normal distribution
   c. Poisson distribution
   b. Moment
   d. Standard deviation

Chapter 9. DIFFERENTIAL EQUATIONS

1. In infinitesimal calculus, a _____ is traditionally an infinitesimally small change in a variable. For example, if x is a variable, then a change in the value of x is often denoted Δx (or δx when this change is considered to be small.) The _____ dx represents such a change, but is infinitely small.

   a. Related rates
   b. Dirichlet integral
   c. Continuous function
   d. Differential

2. A _____ is a mathematical equation for an unknown function of one or several variables that relates the values of the function itself and of its derivatives of various orders. they play a prominent role in engineering, physics, economics and other disciplines.

   A simplified real world example of a _____ is modeling the acceleration of a ball falling through the air (considering only gravity and air resistance.)

   a. Lax pair
   b. Petrovsky lacuna
   c. Structural stability
   d. Differential equation

3. In mathematics, the _____, introduced by German mathematician Georg Cantor in 1883 (but discovered in 1875 by Henry John Stephen Smith), is a set of points lying on a single line segment that has a number of remarkable and deep properties. Through consideration of it, Cantor and others helped lay the foundations of modern general topology. Although Cantor himself defined the set in a general, abstract way, the most common modern construction is the Cantor ternary set, built by removing the middle thirds of a line segment.

   a. BDDC
   b. Planar Lamina
   c. 15 theorem
   d. Cantor set

4. The largest and the smallest element of a set are called extreme values, absolute extrema, or extreme records.

   For a differentiable function f, if $f(x_0)$ is an _____ for the set of all values f(x), and if x_0 is in the interior of the domain of f, then x_0 is a critical point, by Fermat's theorem.

   In the case of a general partial order one should not confuse a least element (smaller than all other) and a minimal element (nothing is smaller.)

   a. Extreme Value Theorem
   b. Extreme Value
   c. Integration by substitution
   d. Infinitesimal

5. In calculus, the _____ states that if a real-valued function f is continuous in the closed and bounded interval [a,b], then f must attain its maximum and minimum value, each at least once. That is, there exist numbers c and d in [a,b] such that:

A related theorem is the boundedness theorem which states that a continuous function f in the closed interval [a,b] is bounded on that interval. That is, there exist real numbers m and M such that:

The _____ enriches the boundedness theorem by saying that not only is the function bounded, but it also attains its least upper bound as its maximum and its greatest lower bound as its minimum.

- a. Infinitesimal
- b. Extreme Value Theorem
- c. Integral of secant cubed
- d. Uniform convergence

6. In mathematics, a _____ is the graph of the system of parametric equations

$$x = A\sin(at + \delta), \quad y = B\sin(bt),$$

which describes complex harmonic motion. This family of curves was investigated by Nathaniel Bowditch in 1815, and later in more detail by Jules Antoine Lissajous in 1857.

The appearance of the figure is highly sensitive to the ratio a/b.

- a. Lissajous curve
- b. BIBO stability
- c. 15 theorem
- d. BDDC

7. The _____ are a pair of first order, non-linear, differential equations frequently used to describe the dynamics of biological systems in which two species interact, one a predator and one its prey. They were proposed independently by Alfred J. Lotka in 1925 and Vito Volterra in 1926.

>

>

where

- y is the number of some predator;
- x is the number of its prey;
- dy/dt and dx/dt represents the growth of the two populations against time;
- t represents the time; and
- >α, >β, >γ and >δ are parameters representing the interaction of the two species.

When multiplied out, the equations take a form useful for physical interpretation. Their origin should be considered from a more general framework,

where both functions represent per capita growth rates of the prey and predator, respectively.

a. Lotka-Volterra equations
b. 15 theorem
c. BIBO stability
d. BDDC

8. The _____ is a polynomial mapping of degree 2, often cited as an archetypal example of how complex, chaotic behaviour can arise from very simple non-linear dynamical equations. The map was popularized in a seminal 1976 paper by the biologist Robert May, in part as a discrete-time demographic model analogous to the logistic equation first created by Pierre François Verhulst. Mathematically, the _____ is written

$$(1) \quad x_{n+1} = rx_n(1 - x_n)$$

where:

x_n is a number between zero and one, and represents the population at year n, and hence x_0 represents the initial population (at year 0)
r is a positive number, and represents a combined rate for reproduction and starvation.

a. 15 theorem
b. Logistic map
c. BIBO stability
d. BDDC

9. The most commonly encountered form of Hooke's law is probably the spring equation, which relates the force exerted by a spring to the distance it is stretched by a _____, k, measured in force per length.

$$F = -kx$$

The negative sign indicates that the force exerted by the spring is in direct opposition to the direction of displacement. It is called a 'restoring force', as it tends to restore the system to equilibrium.

a. Spring constant
b. Polar moment of inertia
c. Navier-Stokes equations
d. 15 theorem

10. In calculus, a branch of mathematics, the _____ is a measurement of how a function changes when its input changes. Loosely speaking, a _____ can be thought of as how much a quantity is changing at some given point. For example, the _____ of the position (or distance) of a vehicle with respect to time is the instantaneous velocity (respectively, instantaneous speed) at which the vehicle is traveling.

Chapter 9. DIFFERENTIAL EQUATIONS

The process of finding a _____ is called differentiation. The fundamental theorem of calculus states that differentiation is the reverse process to integration.

- a. Concave upwards
- b. Mountain pass theorem
- c. Derivative
- d. Ramp function

11. Let f be a differentiable function, and let f'(x) be its derivative. The derivative of f'(x) (if it has one) is written f''(x) and is called the _____ of f. Similarly, the derivative of a _____, if it exists, is written f'''(x) and is called the third derivative of f.

- a. Ramp function
- b. Second Derivative
- c. Horizontal asymptote
- d. Stationary phase approximation

12. In calculus, a branch of mathematics, the _____ is a criterion often useful for determining whether a given stationary point of a function is a local maximum or a local minimum.

The test states: If the function f is twice differentiable at a stationary point x, meaning that $f'(x) = 0$, then:

- If $f''(x) < 0$ then f has a local maximum at x.
- If $f''(x) > 0$ then f has a local minimum at x.
- If $f''(x) = 0$, the _____ says nothing about the point x, has a possible inflection point.

In the last case, the function may have a local maximum or minimum there, but the function is sufficiently 'flat' that this is undetected by the second derivative. In this case one has to examine the third derivative. Such an example is f(x) = x^4.

- a. Metric derivative
- b. Parametric derivative
- c. Stationary point
- d. Second Derivative Test

13. In mathematics, a _____ to an ordinary or partial differential equation is a function for which the derivatives appearing in the equation may not all exist but which is nonetheless deemed to satisfy the equation in some precisely defined sense. There are many different definitions of _____, appropriate for different classes of equations. One of the most important is based on the notion of distributions.

- a. Singular perturbation
- b. Riemann-Hilbert correspondence
- c. Nahm equations
- d. Weak solution

14. In mathematics, in the field of differential equations, an initial value problem is an ordinary differential equation together with specified value, called the _____, of the unknown function at a given point in the domain of the solution. In physics or other sciences, modeling a system frequently amounts to solving an initial value problem; in this context, the differential equation is an evolution equation specifying how, given initial conditions, the system will evolve with time.

An initial value problem is a differential equation

$$y'(t) = f(t, y(t)) \quad \text{with} \quad f : \mathbb{R} \times \mathbb{R} \to \mathbb{R}$$

together with a point in the domain of f

$$(t_0, y_0) \in \mathbb{R} \times \mathbb{R},$$

called the _____.

a. ACTRAN
c. AUSM
b. ALGOR
d. Initial condition

15. In mathematics, in the field of differential equations, an _____ is an ordinary differential equation together with specified value, called the initial condition, of the unknown function at a given point in the domain of the solution. In physics or other sciences, modeling a system frequently amounts to solving an _____; in this context, the differential equation is an evolution equation specifying how, given initial conditions, the system will evolve with time.

An _____ is a differential equation

$$y'(t) = f(t, y(t)) \quad \text{with} \quad f : \mathbb{R} \times \mathbb{R} \to \mathbb{R}$$

together with a point in the domain of f

$$(t_0, y_0) \in \mathbb{R} \times \mathbb{R},$$

called the initial condition.

a. AUSM
c. ACTRAN
b. ALGOR
d. Initial value problem

16. In mathematics, a (topological) _____ is defined as follows: let I be an interval of real numbers (i.e. a non-empty connected subset of $\mathbb{R}$); then a _____ γ is a continuous mapping $\gamma : I \to X$, where X is a topological space. The _____ γ is said to be simple if it is injective, i.e. if for all x, y in I, we have $\gamma(x) = \gamma(y) \implies x = y$. If I is a closed bounded interval $[a, b]$, we also allow the possibility $\gamma(a) = \gamma(b)$ (this convention makes it possible to talk about closed simple _____.)

a. Prolate cycloid
c. Closed curve
b. Tractrix
d. Curve

17. In mathematics, a _____ (or direction field) is a graphical representation of the solutions of a first-order differential equation. It is achieved without solving the differential equation analytically, and thence it is useful. The representation may be used to qualitatively visualise solutions, or to numerically approximate them.

Chapter 9. DIFFERENTIAL EQUATIONS

a. Slope field
c. Fresnel integrals

b. The Method of Mechanical Theorems
d. Standard part function

18.   In mathematics, an autonomous system or _____ is a system of ordinary differential equations which does not depend on the independent variable.

Many laws in physics, where the independent variable is usually assumed to be time, are expressed as autonomous systems because it is assumed the laws of nature which hold now are identical to those for any point in the past or future.

Autonomous systems are closely related to dynamical systems.

a. Integro-differential equation
c. Autonomous differential equation

b. Algebraic differential equation
d. Annihilator method

19.   In mathematics, a _____ differential equation may refer to one of two related things, both of which are differential equations that can be attacked by a method of separation of variables.

- For ordinary differential equations, it describes a class of equations that can be separated into a pair of integrals. See: Examples of differential equations

- For partial differential equations, it describes a class of equations that can be broken down into differential equations in fewer independent variables. See _____ partial differential equation.

a. Lax pair
c. Conserved quantity

b. Weak solution
d. Separable

20.   In mathematics, two vectors are _____ if they are perpendicular, i.e., they form a right angle. For example, a subway and the street above, although they do not physically intersect, are _____ if they cross at a right angle.

a. ACTRAN
c. Orthogonal

b. AUSM
d. ALGOR

21.   In mathematics, _____ are a family of curves in the plane that intersect a given family of curves at right angles. The problem is classical, but is now understood by means of complex analysis; see for example harmonic conjugate.

For a family of level curves described by g(x,y) = C, where C is a constant, the _____ may be found as the level curves of a new function f(x,y) by solving the partial differential equation

$$\nabla f \cdot \nabla g = 0$$

for f(x,y).

Chapter 9. DIFFERENTIAL EQUATIONS

  a. ACTRAN
  c. AUSM

  b. ALGOR
  d. Orthogonal trajectories

22. A _____ is the path a moving object follows through space. The object might be a projectile or a satellite, for example. It thus includes the meaning of orbit - the path of a planet, an asteroid or a comet as it travels around a central mass.
  a. BDDC
  c. BIBO stability

  b. 15 theorem
  d. Trajectory

23. In physics, _____ is defined as the rate of change of position. it is vector physical quantity; both speed and direction are required to define it. In the SI (metric) system, it is measured in meters per second: (m/s) or ms^{-1}.
  a. BDDC
  c. 15 theorem

  b. BIBO stability
  d. Velocity

24. In mathematics, a _____ is a function which preserves the given order. This concept first arose in calculus, and was later generalized to the more abstract setting of order theory.

In calculus, a function f defined on a subset of the real numbers with real values is called monotonic (also monotonically increasing or non-decreasing), if for all x and y such that x >≤ y one has f(x) >≤ f(y), so f preserves the order.

  a. Pettis integral
  c. Monotonic function

  b. 15 theorem
  d. Pseudo-differential operator

25. In mathematics, a _____ is an ordered list of objects (or events). Like a set, it contains members (also called elements or terms), and the number of terms (possibly infinite) is called the length of the _____. Unlike a set, order matters, and the exact same elements can appear multiple times at different positions in the _____.
  a. Y-intercept
  c. Sequence

  b. 15 theorem
  d. BDDC

26. In calculus, the _____ is a shorthand method of finding the derivative of a function that is the reciprocal of a differentiable function, without using the quotient rule or chain rule.

The _____ states that the derivative of 1 / g(x) is given by

$$\frac{d}{dx}\left(\frac{1}{g(x)}\right) = \frac{-g'(x)}{(g(x))^2}$$

where $g(x) \neq 0$.

The _____ is derived from the quotient rule, with the numerator f(x) = 1. Then,

It is also possible to derive the _____ from the chain rule, by a process very much like that of the derivation of the quotient rule.

a. Differentiation rules
c. Quotient Rule

b. Constant factor rule in differentiation
d. Reciprocal Rule

27. A _____ or Gompertz function, named after Benjamin Gompertz, is a sigmoid function. It is a type of mathematical model for a time series, where growth is slowest at the start and end of a time period. Graphs of Gompertz curves, showing the effect of varying one of a,b,c while keeping the others constant.

$$y(t) = ae^{be^{ct}}$$

where

- a is the upper asymptote
- c is the growth rate
- b, c are negative numbers
- e is Euler's Number (e = 2.71828...)

The function curve can be derived from Gompertz's law, which states the rate of mortality (decay) falls exponentially with current size. Mathematically

$$k^r \propto \frac{1}{y(t)}$$

where

- $r = \dfrac{y'(t)}{y(t)}$ is the rate of growth.
- k is an arbitrary constant.

Examples of uses for Gompertz curves include:

- Mobile phone uptake, where costs were initially high (so uptake was slow), followed by a period of rapid growth, followed by a slowing of uptake as saturation was reached.
- Population in a confined space, as birth rates first increase and then slow as resource limits are reached.
- Modeling of growth of tumors

In the sixties A.K. Laird for the first time successfully used the _____ to fit data of growth of tumors. In fact, tumors are cellular populations growing in a confined space where the availability of nutrients is limited.

a. Spheroidal wave functions
c. Gompertz curve

b. Duffing equation
d. Neumann-Dirichlet method

28. In mathematics, the _____ is a criterion for the convergence (a convergence test) of an infinite series

Chapter 9. DIFFERENTIAL EQUATIONS

$$\sum_{n=1}^{\infty} a_n.$$

It is particularly useful in connection with power series.

The _____ was developed first by Cauchy and so is sometimes known as the Cauchy _____ or Cauchy's radical test. The _____ uses the number

$$C = \limsup_{n \to \infty} \sqrt[n]{|a_n|},$$

where 'lim sup' denotes the limit superior, possibly ∞.

    a. Related rates
    c. Binomial series
    b. Dirichlet integral
    d. Root Test

29. _____ is a PDE solver of Maxwell's equations based on the method of moments. It is a 3-D planar electromagnetic (EM) simulator used for passive circuit analysis. It is presently marketed by Agilent Technologies EEsof division , but the tool was original developed by a Belgian company, Alphabit, a spinoff from IMEC, which was acquired by Hewlett-Packard and later spun out as part of Agilent.

    a. Partial Element Equivalent Circuit
    c. Trefftz method
    b. Stencil
    d. Momentum

30. In calculus, the _____ determines whether a given critical point of a function is a maximum, a minimum, or neither.

Suppose that f is a function and we want to determine if f has a maximum or minimum at x. If f is increasing to the left of x and decreasing to the right of x, then x is a local maximum of f.

    a. Test for Divergence
    c. First Derivative Test
    b. Hyperbolic angle
    d. Functional integration

31. In mathematics, the concept of a '_____' is used to describe the behavior of a function as its argument or input either 'gets close' to some point, or as the argument becomes arbitrarily large; or the behavior of a sequence's elements as their index increases indefinitely. Limits are used in calculus and other branches of mathematical analysis to define derivatives and continuity.

In formulas, _____ is usually abbreviated as lim

    a. BDDC
    c. Limit
    b. 15 theorem
    d. BIBO stability

32. In mathematics, a _____ is a differential equation of the form

Chapter 9. DIFFERENTIAL EQUATIONS

$$Ly = f$$

where the differential operator L is a linear operator, y is the unknown function, and the right hand side f is a given function (called the source term.) The linearity condition on L rules out operations such as taking the square of the derivative of y; but permits, for example, taking the second derivative of y. Therefore a fairly general form of such an equation would be

$$a_n(x)D^n y(x) + a_{n-1}(x)D^{n-1}y(x) + \cdots + a_1(x)Dy(x) + a_0(x)y(x) = f(x)$$

where D is the differential operator d/dx (i.e. Dy = y' , D²y = y',...), and the a_i are given functions.

a. Separable
b. Nullcline
c. Linear differential equation
d. Petrovsky lacuna

33. In mathematics, an ordinary differential equation of the form

$$y' + P(x)y = Q(x)y^n$$

is called a _____ when n≠1, 0. Bernoulli equations are special because they are nonlinear differential equations with known exact solutions. Dividing by y^n yields

$$\frac{y'}{y^n} + \frac{P(x)}{y^{n-1}} = Q(x).$$

A change of variables is made to transform into a linear first-order differential equation.

a. Spectral theory of ordinary differential equations
b. Growth curve
c. Separation of variables
d. Bernoulli equation

34. This article will state and prove the _____ for differentiation, and then use it to prove these two formulas.

The _____ for differentiation states that for every natural number n, the derivative of $f(x) = x^n$ is $f'(x) = nx^{n-1}$, that is,

$$(x^n)' = nx^{n-1}.$$

The _____ for integration

$$\int x^n \, dx = \frac{x^{n+1}}{n+1} + C$$

for natural n is then an easy consequence. One just needs to take the derivative of this equality and use the _____ and linearity of differentiation on the right-hand side.

   a. Limits of integration
   c. Power Rule

   b. Dirichlet integral
   d. Hyperbolic angle

35. In mathematics, the point $\tilde{x} \in \mathbb{R}^n$ is an _____ for the differential equation

$$\frac{d\mathbf{x}}{dt} = \mathbf{f}(t, \mathbf{x})$$

if $\mathbf{f}(t, \tilde{\mathbf{x}}) = 0$ for all t.

Similarly, the point $\tilde{x} \in \mathbb{R}^n$ is an _____ (or fixed point) for the difference equation

$$\mathbf{x}_{k+1} = \mathbf{f}(k, \mathbf{x}_k)$$

if $\mathbf{f}(k, \tilde{\mathbf{x}}) = \tilde{\mathbf{x}}$ for $k = 0, 1, 2, \ldots$.

Equilibria can be classified by looking at the signs of the eigenvalues of the linearization of the equations about the equilibria.

   a. AUSM
   c. ACTRAN

   b. ALGOR
   d. Equilibrium point

36. A _____ is a visual display of certain characteristics of certain kinds of differential equations.

Phase planes are useful in visualizing the behavior of physical systems; in particular, of oscillatory systems such as predator-prey models These models can 'spiral in' towards zero, 'spiral out' towards infinity, or reach neutrally stable situations called centres where the path traced out can be either circular, elliptical, or ovoid, or some variant thereof.

   a. Power series method
   c. Phase plane

   b. Separation of variables
   d. Frobenius method

37. A _____ is a geometric representation of the trajectories of a dynamical system in the phase plane. Each set of initial conditions is representated by a different curve, or point.

they are an invaluable tool in studying dynamical systems.

a. BDDC
b. 15 theorem
c. BIBO stability
d. Phase portrait

Chapter 10. PARAMETRIC EQUATIONS AND POLAR COORDINATES

1. In mathematics, the _____ is a conic section, the intersection of a right circular conical surface and a plane parallel to a generating straight line of that surface. Given a point (the focus) and a line (the directrix) that lie in a plane, the locus of points in that plane that are equidistant to them is a _____.

A particular case arises when the plane is tangent to the conical surface of a circle.

    a. 15 theorem   b. BIBO stability
    c. BDDC   d. Parabola

2. In mathematics, _____ are a method of defining a curve. A simple kinematical example is when one uses a time parameter to determine the position, velocity, and other information about a body in motion.

Abstractly, a relation is given in the form of an equation, and it is shown also to be the image of functions from items such as R^n.

    a. Parametric equations   b. Laplace operator
    c. Differential operator   d. Multivariable calculus

3. A _____ or Gompertz function, named after Benjamin Gompertz, is a sigmoid function. It is a type of mathematical model for a time series, where growth is slowest at the start and end of a time period. Graphs of Gompertz curves, showing the effect of varying one of a,b,c while keeping the others constant.

$$y(t) = ae^{be^{ct}}$$

where

- a is the upper asymptote
- c is the growth rate
- b, c are negative numbers
- e is Euler's Number (e = 2.71828...)

The function curve can be derived from Gompertz's law, which states the rate of mortality (decay) falls exponentially with current size. Mathematically

$$k^r \propto \frac{1}{y(t)}$$

where

- $r = \dfrac{y'(t)}{y(t)}$ is the rate of growth.
- k is an arbitrary constant.

Chapter 10. PARAMETRIC EQUATIONS AND POLAR COORDINATES

Examples of uses for Gompertz curves include:

- Mobile phone uptake, where costs were initially high (so uptake was slow), followed by a period of rapid growth, followed by a slowing of uptake as saturation was reached.
- Population in a confined space, as birth rates first increase and then slow as resource limits are reached.
- Modeling of growth of tumors

In the sixties A.K. Laird for the first time successfully used the _____ to fit data of growth of tumors. In fact, tumors are cellular populations growing in a confined space where the availability of nutrients is limited.

   a. Spheroidal wave functions   b. Gompertz curve
   c. Duffing equation   d. Neumann-Dirichlet method

4. In mathematics, a (topological) _____ is defined as follows: let I be an interval of real numbers (i.e. a non-empty connected subset of $\mathbb{R}$); then a _____ γ is a continuous mapping $\gamma : I \to X$, where X is a topological space. The _____ γ is said to be simple if it is injective, i.e. if for all x, y in I, we have $\gamma(x) = \gamma(y) \implies x = y$. If I is a closed bounded interval $[a, b]$, we also allow the possibility $\gamma(a) = \gamma(b)$ (this convention makes it possible to talk about closed simple _____.)

   a. Closed curve   b. Tractrix
   c. Prolate cycloid   d. Curve

5. A _____ is a reference from which measurements are made. In surveying and geodesy, a datum is a set of reference points on the earth's surface against which position measurements are made, and (often) an associated model of the shape of the earth (reference ellipsoid) to define a geographic coordinate system. Horizontal datums are used for describing a point on the earth's surface, in latitude and longitude or another coordinate system.

   a. 15 theorem   b. BIBO stability
   c. BDDC   d. Geodetic datum

6. In the mathematical field of numerical analysis, a _____ is a parametric curve important in computer graphics and related fields. Generalizations of Bezier curves to higher dimensions are called Bezier surfaces, of which the Bezier triangle is a special case.

Bezier curves were widely publicized in 1962 by the French engineer Pierre B>ézier, who used them to design automobile bodies.

   a. BDDC   b. BIBO stability
   c. Bezier curve   d. 15 theorem

7. A _____ is the curve defined by the path of a point on the edge of circular wheel as the wheel rolls along a straight line. It is an example of a roulette, a curve generated by a curve rolling on another curve.

The _____ is the solution to the brachistochrone problem (i.e. it is the curve of fastest descent under gravity) and the related tautochrone problem (i.e. the period of a ball rolling back and forth inside it does not depend on the ball's starting position.)

a. Curtate cycloid
b. Prolate cycloid
c. Tractrix
d. Cycloid

8. The largest and the smallest element of a set are called extreme values, absolute extrema, or extreme records.

For a differentiable function f, if $f(x_0)$ is an _____ for the set of all values f(x), and if x_0 is in the interior of the domain of f, then x_0 is a critical point, by Fermat's theorem.

In the case of a general partial order one should not confuse a least element (smaller than all other) and a minimal element (nothing is smaller.)

a. Infinitesimal
b. Integration by substitution
c. Extreme Value Theorem
d. Extreme Value

9. In calculus, the _____ states that if a real-valued function f is continuous in the closed and bounded interval [a,b], then f must attain its maximum and minimum value, each at least once. That is, there exist numbers c and d in [a,b] such that:

A related theorem is the boundedness theorem which states that a continuous function f in the closed interval [a,b] is bounded on that interval. That is, there exist real numbers m and M such that:

The _____ enriches the boundedness theorem by saying that not only is the function bounded, but it also attains its least upper bound as its maximum and its greatest lower bound as its minimum.

a. Extreme Value Theorem
b. Uniform convergence
c. Integral of secant cubed
d. Infinitesimal

10. A _____ is the curve between two points that is covered in the least time by a body that starts at the first point with zero speed and is constrained to move along the curve to the second point, under the action of constant gravity and assuming no friction.

Given two points A and B, with A not lower than B, there is just one upside down cycloid that passes through A with infinite slope, passes also through B and does not have maximum points between A and B. This particular inverted cycloid is a _____. The curve does not depend on the body's mass or on the strength of the gravitational constant.

a. Prolate cycloid
b. Space curve
c. Closed curve
d. Brachistochrone curve

Chapter 10. PARAMETRIC EQUATIONS AND POLAR COORDINATES

11. A tautochrone or isochrone curve is the curve for which the time taken by an object sliding without friction in uniform gravity to its lowest point is independent of its starting point. The curve is a cycloid, and the time is equal to >π times the square root of the radius over the acceleration of gravity.

The _____, the attempt to identify this curve, was solved by Christiaan Huygens in 1659. He proved geometrically in his Horologium oscillatorium (The Pendulum Clock, 1673) that the curve was a cycloid. This solution was later used to attack the problem of the brachistochrone curve. Jakob Bernoulli solved the problem using calculus in a paper (Acta Eruditorum, 1690) that saw the first published use of the term integral.

a. Folium of Descartes
b. Hypocycloid
c. Tautochrone problem
d. Space curve

12. In a totally ordered set all elements are mutually comparable, so such a set can have at most one minimal element and at most one maximal element. Then, due to mutual comparability, the minimal element will also be the least element and the maximal element will also be the greatest element. Thus in a totally ordered set we can simply use the terms minimum and _____.

a. Maximum
b. Hyperbolic angle
c. Dirichlet integral
d. Complex analysis

13. In calculus, the _____ is a formula for the derivative of the composite of two functions.

In intuitive terms, if a variable, y, depends on a second variable, u, which in turn depends on a third variable, x, then the rate of change of y with respect to x can be computed as the rate of change of y with respect to u multiplied by the rate of change of u with respect to x. Schematically,

$$\frac{dy}{dx} = \frac{dy}{du} \cdot \frac{du}{dx}.$$

a. Chain Rule
b. Quotient Rule
c. Differentiation rules
d. Reciprocal Rule

14. In mathematics, the _____ is a way to approximately calculate the definite integral

$$\int_a^b f(x)\,dx.$$

The _____ works by approximating the region under the graph of the function f by a trapezoid and calculating its area. It follows that

$$\int_a^b f(x)\,dx \approx (b-a)\frac{f(a)+f(b)}{2}.$$

Chapter 10. PARAMETRIC EQUATIONS AND POLAR COORDINATES

To calculate this integral more accurately, one first splits the interval of integration [a,b] into n smaller subintervals, and then applies the _____ on each of them. One obtains the composite _____:

$$\int_a^b f(x)\,dx \approx \frac{b-a}{n}\left[\frac{f(a)+f(b)}{2} + \sum_{k=1}^{n-1} f\left(a + k\frac{b-a}{n}\right)\right].$$

This can alternatively be written as:

$$\int_a^b f(x)\,dx \approx \frac{b-a}{2n}\left(f(x_0) + 2f(x_1) + 2f(x_2) + \cdots + 2f(x_{n-1}) + f(x_n)\right)$$

where

$$x_k = a + k\frac{b-a}{n}, \text{ for } k = 0, 1, \ldots, n$$

(one can also use a non-uniform grid.)

a. 15 theorem
c. BDDC
b. BIBO stability
d. Trapezoidal Rule

15. _____ is the word created by Gilles de Roberval for the curve described by a fixed point as a circle rolls along a straight line. As a circle of radius a rolls without slipping along a line L, the center C moves parallel to L, and every other point P in the rotating plane rigidly attached to the circle traces the curve called the _____. Let CP = b. If P lies inside the circle (b < a), on its circumference (b = a), or outside (b > a), the _____ is described as being curtate, common, or prolate, respectively.

a. Kappa curve
c. Witch of Agnesi
b. Trochoid
d. Hypocycloid

16. In mathematics, the _____ , is the curve defined as follows.

Starting with a fixed circle, a point O on the circle is chosen. For any other point A on the circle, the secant line OA is drawn. The point M is diametrically opposite O. The line OA intersects the tangent at M at the point N. The line parallel to OM through N, and the line perpendicular to OM through A intersect at P. As the point A is varied, the path of P is the witch.

a. Cochleoid
c. Closed curve
b. Witch of Agnesi
d. Folium of Descartes

17. In mathematics, a _____ is the graph of the system of parametric equations

$$x = A\sin(at + \delta), \quad y = B\sin(bt),$$

which describes complex harmonic motion. This family of curves was investigated by Nathaniel Bowditch in 1815, and later in more detail by Jules Antoine Lissajous in 1857.

The appearance of the figure is highly sensitive to the ratio a/b.

    a. BDDC   b. Lissajous curve
    c. BIBO stability   d. 15 theorem

18.   In calculus, the _____ is a formula used to find the derivatives of products of functions. It may be stated thus:

$$(f \cdot g)' = f' \cdot g + f \cdot g'$$

or in the Leibniz notation thus:

$$\frac{d}{dx}(u \cdot v) = u \cdot \frac{dv}{dx} + v \cdot \frac{du}{dx}.$$

Discovery of this rule is credited to Gottfried Leibniz, who demonstrated it using differentials. Here is Leibniz's argument: Let u and v be two differentiable functions of x.

    a. Constant factor rule in differentiation   b. Product Rule
    c. Reciprocal Rule   d. Quotient Rule

19.   In mathematics, an _____ is a particular type of curve: a hypocycloid with four cusps. Astroids are also superellipses: all astroids are scaled versions of the curve specified by the equation

$$x^{2/3} + y^{2/3} = 1.$$

Its modern name comes from the Greek word for 'star'.

    a. Epicycloid   b. ACTRAN
    c. ALGOR   d. Astroid

20.   An _____ of a real-valued function y = f(x) is a curve which describes the behavior of f as either x or y tends to infinity.

In other words, as one moves along the graph of f(x) in some direction, the distance between it and the _____ eventually becomes smaller than any distance that one may specify.

a. AUSM b. Asymptote
c. ACTRAN d. ALGOR

21. In geometry, a _____ is a special plane curve generated by the trace of a fixed point on a small circle that rolls within a larger circle. It is comparable to the cycloid but instead of the circle rolling along a line, it rolls within a circle. The red curve is a _____ traced as the smaller black circle rolls around inside the larger blue circle (parameters are R=3.0, r=1.0, and so k=3), giving a deltoid.

If the smaller circle has radius r, and the larger circle has radius R = kr, then the parametric equations for the curve can be given by either:

$$x(\theta) = (R-r)\cos\theta + r\cos\left(\frac{R-r}{r}\theta\right)$$
$$y(\theta) = (R-r)\sin\theta - r\sin\left(\frac{R-r}{r}\theta\right),$$

or:

$$x(\theta) = r(k-1)\cos\theta + r\cos((k-1)\theta)$$
$$y(\theta) = r(k-1)\sin\theta - r\sin((k-1)\theta).$$

If k is an integer, then the curve is closed, and has k cusps (i.e., sharp corners, where the curve is not differentiable.)

a. Closed curve b. Kappa curve
c. Bullet-nose curve d. Hypocycloid

22. In geometry, an _____ is a plane curve produced by tracing the path of a chosen point of a circle -- called epicycle -- which rolls without slipping around a fixed circle. It is a particular kind of roulette.

If the smaller circle has radius r, and the larger circle has radius R = kr, then the parametric equations for the curve can be given by either:

$$x(\theta) = (R+r)\cos\theta - r\cos\left(\frac{R+r}{r}\theta\right)$$
$$y(\theta) = (R+r)\sin\theta - r\sin\left(\frac{R+r}{r}\theta\right),$$

or:

$$x(\theta) = r(k+1)\cos\theta - r\cos((k+1)\theta)$$
$$y(\theta) = r(k+1)\sin\theta - r\sin((k+1)\theta).$$

If k is an integer, then the curve is closed, and has k cusps (i.e., sharp corners, where the curve is not differentiable.)

a. Epicycloid
b. Asymptotic curve
c. ACTRAN
d. ALGOR

23. In calculus, _____, was originally the use of expressions such as dx and dy and to represent 'infinitely small' (or infinitesimal) increments of quantities x and y, just as >Δx and >Δy represent finite increments of x and y respectively. So for y being a function of x, or

the derivative of y with respect to x, which later came to be viewed as

was, according to Leibniz, the quotient of an infinitesimal increment of y by an infinitesimal increment of x, or

where the right hand side is Lagrange's notation for the derivative of f at x.

Similarly, although mathematicians usually now view an integral

as a limit

where >Δx is an interval containing x_i, Leibniz viewed it as the sum (the integral sign denoting summation) of infinitely many infinitesimal quantities f(x) dx.

a. Leibniz's notation
b. Fermat differentiation
c. Gradient
d. Notation for differentiation

24. For some curves there is a smallest number L that is an upper bound on the length of any polygonal approximation. If such a number exists, then the curve is said to be rectifiable and the curve is defined to have _____ L.

Let C be a curve in Euclidean (or, generally, a metric) space $X = R^n$, so C is the image of a continuous function $f : [a, b] \to X$ of the interval [a, b] into X.

    a. Integration by parametric derivatives
    b. Integrand
    c. Order of integration
    d. Arc length

25. A _____ is a surface in the Euclidean space R^3 which is defined by a parametric equation with two parameters. Parametric representation is the most general way to specify a surface. Surfaces that occur in two of the main theorems of vector calculus, Stokes' theorem and divergence theorem, are frequently given in a parametric form.

    a. PDE surfaces
    b. Paraboloid
    c. Parametric surface
    d. Normal line

26. In mathematics and its applications, a _____ system is a system for assigning an n-tuple of numbers or scalars to each point in an n-dimensional space. This concept is part of the theory of manifolds. 'Scalars' in many cases means real numbers, but, depending on context, can mean complex numbers or elements of some other commutative ring.

    a. Coordinate
    b. Cylindrical coordinate system
    c. Spherical coordinate system
    d. 15 theorem

27. In mathematics, _____ refers to any of a number of loosely related concepts in different areas of geometry. Intuitively, _____ is the amount by which a geometric object deviates from being flat, or straight in the case of a line, but this is defined in different ways depending on the context. There is a key distinction between extrinsic _____, which is defined for objects embedded in another space (usually a Euclidean space) in a way that relates to the radius of _____ of circles that touch the object, and intrinsic _____, which is defined at each point in a differential manifold.

    a. Curvature
    b. Tangent line
    c. Lie derivative
    d. Tortuosity

28. In mathematics, the _____ is a two-dimensional coordinate system in which each point on a plane is determined by an angle and a distance. The _____ is especially useful in situations where the relationship between two points is most easily expressed in terms of angles and distance; in the more familiar Cartesian or rectangular coordinate system, such a relationship can only be found through trigonometric formulation.

As the coordinate system is two-dimensional, each point is determined by two polar coordinates: the radial coordinate and the angular coordinate.

    a. Polar coordinate system
    b. 15 theorem
    c. BDDC
    d. BIBO stability

29. In complex analysis, a mathematical discipline, a _____ of a meromorphic function is a certain type of singularity that behaves like the singularity of $\frac{1}{z^n}$ at z = 0. This means that, in particular, a _____ of the function f(z) is a point z = a such that f(z) approaches infinity uniformly as z approaches a.

Formally, suppose U is an open subset of the complex plane C, a is an element of U and $f : U \setminus \{a\} \to C$ is a function which is holomorphic over its domain.

Chapter 10. PARAMETRIC EQUATIONS AND POLAR COORDINATES

a. Pole
c. Holomorphic function

b. Removable singularity
d. Regular part

30. The _____ are a pair of first order, non-linear, differential equations frequently used to describe the dynamics of biological systems in which two species interact, one a predator and one its prey. They were proposed independently by Alfred J. Lotka in 1925 and Vito Volterra in 1926.

where

- y is the number of some predator;
- x is the number of its prey;
- dy/dt and dx/dt represents the growth of the two populations against time;
- t represents the time; and
- >α, >β, >γ and >δ are parameters representing the interaction of the two species.

When multiplied out, the equations take a form useful for physical interpretation. Their origin should be considered from a more general framework,

where both functions represent per capita growth rates of the prey and predator, respectively.

a. BDDC
c. BIBO stability

b. 15 theorem
d. Lotka-Volterra equations

31. In mathematics, the _____, introduced by German mathematician Georg Cantor in 1883 (but discovered in 1875 by Henry John Stephen Smith), is a set of points lying on a single line segment that has a number of remarkable and deep properties. Through consideration of it, Cantor and others helped lay the foundations of modern general topology. Although Cantor himself defined the set in a general, abstract way, the most common modern construction is the Cantor ternary set, built by removing the middle thirds of a line segment.

a. BDDC
c. Planar Lamina

b. Cantor set
d. 15 theorem

32. In mathematics, a _____ decomposes a periodic function into a sum of simple oscillating functions, namely sines and cosines (or complex exponentials.) The study of _____ is a branch of Fourier analysis. _____ were introduced by Joseph Fourier (1768-1830) for the purpose of solving the heat equation in a metal plate.

Chapter 10. PARAMETRIC EQUATIONS AND POLAR COORDINATES

a. Fourier series
c. 15 theorem
b. BIBO stability
d. BDDC

33. A _____ is closed curve with one cusp.

In geometry, the _____ is an epicycloid with one cusp.

Rolling circle around another fixed circle produces _____ (red curve) Conformal mapping from circle to _____

- epicycloid produced as the path (or locus) of a point on the circumference of a circle as that circle rolls around another fixed circle with the same radius.

- limaçon with one cusp. The cusp is formed when the ratio of a to b in the equation is equal to one.

a. BIBO stability
c. Cardioid
b. 15 theorem
d. BDDC

34. In mathematics, a _____ or rhodonea curve is a sinusoid plotted in polar coordinates. Up to similarity, these curves can all be expressed by a polar equation of the form

$$r = \cos(k\theta).$$

If k is an integer, the curve will be _____ shaped with

- 2k petals if k is even, and
- k petals if k is odd.

When k is even, the entire graph of the _____ will be traced out exactly once when the value of θ changes from 0 to 2π. When k is odd, this will happen on the interval between 0 and π. (More generally, this will happen on any interval of length 2π for k even, and π for k odd.)

a. Curtate cycloid
c. Space curve
b. Cochleoid
d. Rose

35. In mathematics, a _____ is a set (or locus) of points in the plane such that each point p on the oval bears a special relation to two other, fixed points q_1 and q_2: the product of the distance from p to q_1 and the distance from p to q_2 is constant. That is, if we define the function dist(x,y) to be the distance from a point x to a point y, then all points p on a _____ satisfy the equation

$$\text{dist}(q_1, p) \times \text{dist}(q_2, p) = b^2$$

where b is a constant.

The points q_1 and q_2 are called the foci of the oval.

    a. Folium of Descartes
    b. Secant line
    c. Tractrix
    d. Cassini oval

36. In calculus, a branch of mathematics, the _____ is a measurement of how a function changes when its input changes. Loosely speaking, a _____ can be thought of as how much a quantity is changing at some given point. For example, the _____ of the position (or distance) of a vehicle with respect to time is the instantaneous velocity (respectively, instantaneous speed) at which the vehicle is traveling.

The process of finding a _____ is called differentiation. The fundamental theorem of calculus states that differentiation is the reverse process to integration.

    a. Mountain pass theorem
    b. Concave upwards
    c. Ramp function
    d. Derivative

37. Let f be a differentiable function, and let f'(x) be its derivative. The derivative of f'(x) (if it has one) is written f''(x) and is called the _____ of f. Similarly, the derivative of a _____, if it exists, is written f'''(x) and is called the third derivative of f.

    a. Stationary phase approximation
    b. Second Derivative
    c. Horizontal asymptote
    d. Ramp function

38. In calculus, a branch of mathematics, the _____ is a criterion often useful for determining whether a given stationary point of a function is a local maximum or a local minimum.

The test states: If the function f is twice differentiable at a stationary point x, meaning that $f'(x) = 0$, then:

- If $f''(x) < 0$ then f has a local maximum at x.
- If $f''(x) > 0$ then f has a local minimum at x.
- If $f''(x) = 0$, the _____ says nothing about the point x, has a possible inflection point.

In the last case, the function may have a local maximum or minimum there, but the function is sufficiently 'flat' that this is undetected by the second derivative. In this case one has to examine the third derivative. Such an example is $f(x) = x^4$.

    a. Stationary point
    b. Parametric derivative
    c. Metric derivative
    d. Second Derivative Test

39. In calculus, the _____ is a theorem regarding the limit of a function.

The _____ is a technical result which is very important in proofs in calculus and mathematical analysis. It is typically used to confirm the limit of a function via comparison with two other functions whose limits are known or easily computed.

a. 15 theorem
b. Table of limits
c. Limit of a sequence
d. Squeeze Theorem

40. A _____ is a cubic curve generated by increasing or diminishing the radius vector of a variable point P on a straight line by the distance PA of the point from the foot of the perpendicular drawn from the origin to the fixed line.

The polar equation is

$$r = a \cos 2\theta \sec \theta.$$

The Cartesian equation is

$y^2 = x^2 /$,

where a is the distance of the line from the origin.

a. Tschirnhausen cubic
b. Macbeath surface
c. Strophoid
d. Kampyle of Eudoxus

41. In mathematics, a _____ (or just conic) is a curve obtained by intersecting a cone (more precisely, a circular conical surface) with a plane. A _____ is therefore a restriction of a quadric surface to the plane. The conic sections were named and studied as long ago as 200 BC, when Apollonius of Perga undertook a systematic study of their properties.

a. BDDC
b. Conic section
c. Foci
d. 15 theorem

42. In mathematics, an _____, is the apparent shape of a circle viewed obliquely from outside it, as distinct from a hyperbola which is the shape seen from inside. It is the finite or bounded case of a conic section as a shape cut in a cone by a plane, the unbounded cases being the parabola, which like the _____ remains connected, and the hyperbola, which separates into two connected components or branches.

Equivalently an _____ can be defined as the locus of points, or path traced out, in a plane such that the sum of the distances from the moving point to two fixed points remains constant.

a. ACTRAN
b. ALGOR
c. Ellipse
d. AUSM

43. In geometry, the _____, pronounced , are a pair of special points used in describing conic sections. The four types of conic sections are the circle, parabola, ellipse, and hyperbola.

The focus has two equivalent defining properties; and they always fall on the major axis of symmetry of the conic.

Chapter 10. PARAMETRIC EQUATIONS AND POLAR COORDINATES

    a. Latus rectum   b. BDDC
    c. Foci   d. 15 theorem

44. In mathematics, the _____ is a representation of a function as an infinite sum of terms calculated from the values of its derivatives at a single point. It may be regarded as the limit of the Taylor polynomials. If the series is centered at zero, the series is also called a Maclaurin series.

    a. Taylor series   b. BIBO stability
    c. 15 theorem   d. BDDC

45. The _____ is a test to determine if a relation or its graph is a function or not. For a relation or graph to be a function, it can have at most a single y-value for each x-value. Thus, a vertical line drawn at any x-position on the graph of a function will intersect the graph at most once.

    a. 15 theorem   b. BIBO stability
    c. Vertical Line Test   d. BDDC

46. In infinitesimal calculus, a _____ is traditionally an infinitesimally small change in a variable. For example, if x is a variable, then a change in the value of x is often denoted Δx (or δx when this change is considered to be small.) The _____ dx represents such a change, but is infinitely small.

    a. Related rates   b. Dirichlet integral
    c. Continuous function   d. Differential

47. In geometry, the _____ (also semimajor axis) is used to describe the dimensions of ellipses and hyperbolae.

The major axis of an ellipse is its longest diameter, a line that runs through the centre and both foci, its ends being at the widest points of the shape. The _____ is one half of the major axis, and thus runs from the centre, through a focus, and to the edge of the ellipse.

    a. BIBO stability   b. BDDC
    c. 15 theorem   d. Semi-major axis

48. In calculus, the _____ is a shorthand method of finding the derivative of a function that is the reciprocal of a differentiable function, without using the quotient rule or chain rule.

The _____ states that the derivative of 1 / g(x) is given by

$$\frac{d}{dx}\left(\frac{1}{g(x)}\right) = \frac{-g'(x)}{(g(x))^2}$$

where $g(x) \neq 0$.

The _____ is derived from the quotient rule, with the numerator f(x) = 1. Then,

      It is also possible to derive the _____ from the chain rule, by a process very much like that of the derivation of the quotient rule.

a. Differentiation rules
b. Reciprocal Rule
c. Constant factor rule in differentiation
d. Quotient Rule

49. In mathematics, an _____ is an infinite series of the form

$$\sum_{n=0}^{\infty} (-1)^n a_n,$$

with $a_n \geq 0$ (or $a_n \leq 0$) for all n. A finite sum of this kind is an alternating sum. An _____ converges if the terms a_n converge to 0 monotonically.

a. Uniform convergence
b. Alternating Series
c. Infinite series
d. Extreme value

50. Derivative terms are used to identify the body being orbited. The most common are perigee and apogee, referring to orbits around the Earth, and perihelion and _____, referring to orbits around the Sun. During the Apollo program, the terms pericynthion and apocynthion were used when referring to the moon.

a. Aphelion
b. ACTRAN
c. AUSM
d. ALGOR

51. A _____ is a snail-shaped curve similar to a strophoid which can be represented by the polar equation

$$r = \frac{a \sin \theta}{\theta}$$

the Cartesian equation

$$(x^2 + y^2) \arctan \frac{y}{x} = ay$$

or the parametric equations

$$x = \frac{a \sin t \cos t}{t}$$
$$y = \frac{a \sin^2 t}{t}$$

a. Tautochrone problem
b. Secant line
c. Hypocycloid
d. Cochleoid

52. In Geometry, the _____ is an algebraic curve defined by the equation

$$x^3 + y^3 - 3axy = 0$$

It forms a loop in the first quadrant with a double point at the origin and asymptote

$$x + y + a = 0$$

It is symmetrical about y = x.

a. Prolate cycloid
b. Cochleoid
c. Folium of Descartes
d. Curve

Chapter 11. INFINITE SEQUENCES AND SERIES

1. In mathematics, a _____ is an ordered list of objects (or events). Like a set, it contains members (also called elements or terms), and the number of terms (possibly infinite) is called the length of the _____. Unlike a set, order matters, and the exact same elements can appear multiple times at different positions in the _____.

   a. 15 theorem
   b. Y-intercept
   c. BDDC
   d. Sequence

2. In calculus, a branch of mathematics, the _____ is a measurement of how a function changes when its input changes. Loosely speaking, a _____ can be thought of as how much a quantity is changing at some given point. For example, the _____ of the position (or distance) of a vehicle with respect to time is the instantaneous velocity (respectively, instantaneous speed) at which the vehicle is traveling.

   The process of finding a _____ is called differentiation. The fundamental theorem of calculus states that differentiation is the reverse process to integration.

   a. Concave upwards
   b. Mountain pass theorem
   c. Ramp function
   d. Derivative

3. In mathematics, the concept of a '_____' is used to describe the behavior of a function as its argument or input either 'gets close' to some point, or as the argument becomes arbitrarily large; or the behavior of a sequence's elements as their index increases indefinitely. Limits are used in calculus and other branches of mathematical analysis to define derivatives and continuity.

   In formulas, _____ is usually abbreviated as lim

   a. BIBO stability
   b. BDDC
   c. 15 theorem
   d. Limit

4. Let f be a differentiable function, and let f'(x) be its derivative. The derivative of f'(x) (if it has one) is written f''(x) and is called the _____ of f. Similarly, the derivative of a _____, if it exists, is written f'''(x) and is called the third derivative of f.

   a. Ramp function
   b. Second Derivative
   c. Horizontal asymptote
   d. Stationary phase approximation

5. In calculus, a branch of mathematics, the _____ is a criterion often useful for determining whether a given stationary point of a function is a local maximum or a local minimum.

   The test states: If the function f is twice differentiable at a stationary point x, meaning that $f'(x) = 0$, then:

   - If $f''(x) < 0$ then f has a local maximum at x.
   - If $f''(x) > 0$ then f has a local minimum at x.
   - If $f''(x) = 0$, the _____ says nothing about the point x, has a possible inflection point.

   In the last case, the function may have a local maximum or minimum there, but the function is sufficiently 'flat' that this is undetected by the second derivative. In this case one has to examine the third derivative. Such an example is f(x) = x⁴.

Chapter 11. INFINITE SEQUENCES AND SERIES

a. Metric derivative
c. Parametric derivative
b. Stationary point
d. Second Derivative Test

6. In probability theory, a probability distribution is called continuous if its cumulative distribution function is continuous. This is equivalent to saying that for random variables X with the distribution in question, Pr[X = a] = 0 for all real numbers a, i.e.: the probability that X attains the value a is zero, for any number a. If the distribution of X is continuous then X is called a _____.

a. Standard deviation
c. Linear regression
b. Moment
d. Continuous random variable

7. In calculus, the _____ is a theorem regarding the limit of a function.

The _____ is a technical result which is very important in proofs in calculus and mathematical analysis. It is typically used to confirm the limit of a function via comparison with two other functions whose limits are known or easily computed.

a. Limit of a sequence
c. Table of limits
b. 15 theorem
d. Squeeze Theorem

8. A _____ or Gompertz function, named after Benjamin Gompertz, is a sigmoid function. It is a type of mathematical model for a time series, where growth is slowest at the start and end of a time period. Graphs of Gompertz curves, showing the effect of varying one of a,b,c while keeping the others constant.

$$y(t) = ae^{be^{ct}}$$

where

- a is the upper asymptote
- c is the growth rate
- b, c are negative numbers
- e is Euler's Number (e = 2.71828...)

The function curve can be derived from Gompertz's law, which states the rate of mortality (decay) falls exponentially with current size. Mathematically

$$k^r \propto \frac{1}{y(t)}$$

where

- $r = \dfrac{y'(t)}{y(t)}$ is the rate of growth.
- k is an arbitrary constant.

Examples of uses for Gompertz curves include:

- Mobile phone uptake, where costs were initially high (so uptake was slow), followed by a period of rapid growth, followed by a slowing of uptake as saturation was reached.
- Population in a confined space, as birth rates first increase and then slow as resource limits are reached.
- Modeling of growth of tumors

In the sixties A.K. Laird for the first time successfully used the _____ to fit data of growth of tumors. In fact, tumors are cellular populations growing in a confined space where the availability of nutrients is limited.

a. Spheroidal wave functions
c. Gompertz curve

b. Duffing equation
d. Neumann-Dirichlet method

9. In mathematics, a _____ is a function which preserves the given order. This concept first arose in calculus, and was later generalized to the more abstract setting of order theory.

In calculus, a function f defined on a subset of the real numbers with real values is called monotonic (also monotonically increasing or non-decreasing), if for all x and y such that x >≤ y one has f(x) >≤ f(y), so f preserves the order.

a. 15 theorem
c. Pettis integral

b. Monotonic function
d. Pseudo-differential operator

Chapter 11. INFINITE SEQUENCES AND SERIES

10. In elementary algebra, a _____ is a polynomial with two terms--the sum of two monomials--often bound by parenthesis or brackets when operated upon. It is the simplest kind of polynomial other than monomials.

- The _____ $a^2 - b^2$ can be factored as the product of two other binomials:

    $a^2 - b^2 = (a + b)(a - b.)$

    This is a special case of the more general formula:
    $$a^{n+1} - b^{n+1} = (a-b)\sum_{k=0}^{n} a^k b^{n-k}.$$

- The product of a pair of linear binomials $(ax + b)$ and $(cx + d)$ is:

    $(ax + b)(cx + d) = acx^2 + axd + bcx + bd.$

- A _____ raised to the nth power, represented as

    $(a + b)^n$

    can be expanded by means of the _____ theorem or, equivalently, using Pascal's triangle. Taking a simple example, the perfect square _____ $(p + q)^2$ can be found by squaring the :first digit, adding twice the product of the first and second digit and finally adding the square of the second digit, to give $p^2 + 2pq + q^2$.

a. Completing the square
b. Partial fractions
c. Binomial
d. Multinomial theorem

11. In mathematics, the _____ is an important formula giving the expansion of powers of sums. Its simplest version states that

$$(x+y)^n = \sum_{k=0}^{n} \binom{n}{k} x^{n-k} y^k \qquad (1)$$

for any real or complex numbers x and y, and any non-negative integer n. The binomial coefficient appearing in (1) may be defined in terms of the factorial function n!:

$$\binom{n}{k} = \frac{n!}{k!\,(n-k)!}.$$

For example, here are the cases where 2 ≤ n ≤ 5:

$$(x+y)^2 = x^2 + 2xy + y^2$$
$$(x+y)^3 = x^3 + 3x^2y + 3xy^2 + y^3$$
$$(x+y)^4 = x^4 + 4x^3y + 6x^2y^2 + 4xy^3 + y^4$$
$$(x+y)^5 = x^5 + 5x^4y + 10x^3y^2 + 10x^2y^3 + 5xy^4 + y^5.$$

Formula (1) is valid more generally for any elements x and y of a semiring as long as xy = yx.

a. Trinomial expansion   b. Binomial Theorem
c. Stirling transform   d. Lah numbers

12. In mathematics, a function f defined on some set X with real or complex values is a _____ function, if the set of its values is _____. In other words, there exists a number M>0 such that

$$|f(x)| \leq M$$

for all x in X.

Sometimes, if $f(x) \leq A$ for all x in X, then the function is said to be _____ above by A.

a. Stationary phase approximation   b. Bounded
c. Differential calculus   d. Caccioppoli set

13. In mathematics, given a subset S of a partially ordered set T, the _____ (sup) of S, if it exists, is the least element of T that is greater than or equal to each element of S. Consequently, the _____ is also referred to as the least upper bound, lub or LUB. If the _____ exists, it may or may not belong to S.

a. 15 theorem   b. Supremum
c. BIBO stability   d. BDDC

14. In calculus, the _____ allows you to take constants outside a derivative and concentrate on differentiating the function of x itself. This is a part of the linearity of differentiation.

Suppose you have a function

$$g(x) = k \cdot f(x).$$

where k is a constant.

Use the formula for differentiation from first principles to obtain:

$$g'(x) = \lim_{h \to 0} \frac{g(x+h) - g(x)}{h}$$
$$g'(x) = \lim_{h \to 0} \frac{k \cdot f(x+h) - k \cdot f(x)}{h}$$
$$g'(x) = \lim_{h \to 0} \frac{k(f(x+h) - f(x))}{h}$$
$$g'(x) = k \lim_{h \to 0} \frac{f(x+h) - f(x)}{h} \quad (*)$$
$$g'(x) = k \cdot f'(x).$$

This is the statement of the _____, in Lagrange's notation for differentiation.

a. Product rule
b. Constant factor rule in differentiation
c. Differentiation rules
d. Reciprocal Rule

15. In mathematics, the _____ of two positive real numbers x and y is defined as follows:

First compute the arithmetic mean of x and y and call it a_1. Next compute the geometric mean of x and y and call it g_1; this is the square root of the product xy:

$$a_1 = \frac{x+y}{2}$$
$$g_1 = \sqrt{xy}.$$

Then iterate this operation with a_1 taking the place of x and g_1 taking the place of y. In this way, two sequences (a_n) and (g_n) are defined:

$$a_{n+1} = \frac{a_n + g_n}{2}$$
$$g_{n+1} = \sqrt{a_n g_n}.$$

These two sequences converge to the same number, which is the _____ of x and y; it is denoted by M(x, y), or sometimes by agm(x, y.)

a. ALGOR   b. AUSM
c. ACTRAN   d. Arithmetic-geometric mean

16. In mathematics, a _____ is an expression such as

$$x = a_0 + \cfrac{1}{a_1 + \cfrac{1}{a_2 + \cfrac{1}{a_3 + \cfrac{1}{\ddots}}}}$$

where a_0 is an integer and all the other numbers a_i ($i \neq 0$) are positive integers. Longer expressions are defined analogously. If the partial numerators and partial denominators are allowed to assume arbitrary values, which may in some contexts include functions, the resulting expression is a generalized _____.

a. Restricted partial quotients   b. Periodic continued fraction
c. Stern-Brocot tree   d. Continued fraction

17. In probability theory and statistics, the _____ (or expectation value or mean and for continuous random variables with a density function it is the probability density -weighted integral of the possible values.

The term '_____' can be misleading.

a. ALGOR   b. ACTRAN
c. AUSM   d. Expected value

18. In mathematics, a _____ is the graph of the system of parametric equations

$$x = A\sin(at + \delta), \quad y = B\sin(bt),$$

which describes complex harmonic motion. This family of curves was investigated by Nathaniel Bowditch in 1815, and later in more detail by Jules Antoine Lissajous in 1857.

The appearance of the figure is highly sensitive to the ratio a/b.

a. BIBO stability   b. BDDC
c. Lissajous curve   d. 15 theorem

19. Cantor defined two kinds of _____ numbers, the ordinal numbers and the cardinal numbers. Ordinal numbers may be identified with well-ordered sets, or counting carried on to any stopping point, including points after an _____ number have already been counted. Generalizing finite and the ordinary _____ sequences which are maps from the positive integers leads to mappings from ordinal numbers, and transfinite sequences.

a. Infinite
c. AUSM
b. ALGOR
d. ACTRAN

20.   In mathematics, a _____ is an infinite series that is not convergent, meaning that the infinite sequence of the partial sums of the series does not have a limit.

If a series converges, the individual terms of the series must approach zero. Thus any series in which the individual terms do not approach zero diverges.

   a. Divergent series
   c. BIBO stability
b. 15 theorem
d. BDDC

21.   In mathematics, a _____ is a series with a constant ratio between successive terms. For example, the series

$$\frac{1}{2} + \frac{1}{4} + \frac{1}{8} + \frac{1}{16} + \cdots$$

is geometric, because each term is equal to half of the previous term. The sum of this series is 1, as illustrated in the following picture:

_____ are one of the simplest examples of infinite series with finite sums.

   a. Converge absolutely
   c. Sequence transformation
b. Telescoping series
d. Geometric series

22.   The terms of the series are often produced according to a certain rule, such as by a formula, by an algorithm, by a sequence of measurements, or even by a random number generator. As there are an infinite number of terms, this notion is often called an _____. Unlike finite summations, series need tools from mathematical analysis to be fully understood and manipulated.
   a. Extreme value
   c. Extreme Value Theorem
b. Integration by substitution
d. Infinite series

23.   Call S_N the _____ to N of the sequence $\{a_n\}$, or _____ of the series. A series is the sequence of partial sums, $\{S_N\}$.

When talking about series, one can refer either to the sequence $\{S_N\}$ of the partial sums, or to the sum of the series,

$$\sum_{n=0}^{\infty} a_n$$

i.e., the limit of the sequence of partial sums - it is clear which one is meant from context.

a. Minimum
b. Root test
c. Partial sum
d. Periodic function

24. A _____ is an expression which compares quantities relative to each other. The most common examples involve two quantities, but in theory any number of quantities can be compared. In mathematical terms, they are represented by separating each quantity with a colon, for example the _____ 2:3, which is read as the _____ 'two to three'.
   a. Sequence
   b. 15 theorem
   c. BDDC
   d. Ratio

25. In acoustics and telecommunication, a _____ of a wave is a component frequency of the signal that is an integer multiple of the fundamental frequency. For example, if the fundamental frequency is f, the harmonics have frequencies f, 2f, 3f, 4f, etc. The harmonics have the property that they are all periodic at the fundamental frequency, therefore the sum of harmonics is also periodic at that frequency.
   a. BDDC
   b. 15 theorem
   c. Harmonic
   d. BIBO stability

26. In mathematics, the _____ is the infinite series

$$\sum_{k=1}^{\infty} \frac{1}{k} = 1 + \frac{1}{2} + \frac{1}{3} + \frac{1}{4} + \cdots.$$

Its name derives from the concept of overtones, or harmonics, in music: the wavelengths of the overtones of a vibrating string are 1/2, 1/3, 1/4, etc., of the string's fundamental wavelength. Every term of the series after the first is the harmonic mean of the neighboring terms; the term harmonic mean likewise derives from music.

The _____ diverges to infinity, albeit rather slowly (the first 10^{43} terms sum to less than 100 .)

   a. BDDC
   b. 15 theorem
   c. BIBO stability
   d. Harmonic series

27. In mathematics, a _____ is an informal expression referring to a series whose sum can be found by exploiting the circumstance that nearly every term cancels with either a succeeding or preceding term. Such a technique is also known as the method of differences.

For example, the series

$$\sum_{n=1}^{\infty} \frac{1}{n(n+1)}$$

simplifies as

$$\sum_{n=1}^{\infty} \frac{1}{n(n+1)} = \sum_{n=1}^{\infty} \left(\frac{1}{n} - \frac{1}{n+1}\right)$$
$$= \left(1 - \frac{1}{2}\right) + \left(\frac{1}{2} - \frac{1}{3}\right) + \cdots$$
$$= 1 + \left(-\frac{1}{2} + \frac{1}{2}\right) + \left(-\frac{1}{3} + \frac{1}{3}\right) + \cdots = 1.$$

Chapter 11. INFINITE SEQUENCES AND SERIES

Although telescoping can be a useful technique, there are pitfalls to watch out for:

$$0 = \sum_{n=1}^{\infty} 0 = \sum_{n=1}^{\infty}(1-1) = 1 + \sum_{n=1}^{\infty}(-1+1) = 1$$

is not correct because regrouping of terms is invalid unless the individual terms converge to 0; see Grandi's series.

 a. Geometric series
 b. Sequence transformation
 c. Converge absolutely
 d. Telescoping series

28. In vector calculus, the _____ is an operator that measures the magnitude of a vector field's source or sink at a given point; the _____ of a vector field is a (signed) scalar. For example, consider air as it is heated or cooled. The relevant vector field for this example is the velocity of the moving air at a point.
 a. Gradient theorem
 b. Divergence Theorem
 c. Triple product
 d. Divergence

29. In mathematics, the nth term _____ is a simple test for the divergence of an infinite series:

- If $\lim_{n \to \infty} a_n \neq 0$ or if the limit does not exist, then $\sum_{n=1}^{\infty} a_n$ diverges.

Many authors do not name this test or give it a shorter name.

Unlike stronger convergence tests, the term test cannot prove by itself that a series converges. In particular, the converse to the test is not true; instead all one can say is:

- If $\lim_{n \to \infty} a_n = 0$, then $\sum_{n=1}^{\infty} a_n$ may or may not converge. In other words, if $\lim_{n \to \infty} a_n = 0$, the test is inconclusive.

The harmonic series is a classic example of a divergent series whose terms limit to zero. The more general class of p-series,

$$\sum_{n=1}^{\infty} \frac{1}{n^p},$$

Chapter 11. INFINITE SEQUENCES AND SERIES

exemplifies the possible results of the test:

- If p ≤ 0, then the term test identifies the series as divergent.
- If 0 < p ≤ 1, then the term test is inconclusive, but the series is divergent by the integral test for convergence.
- If 1 < p, then the term test is inconclusive, but the series is convergent, again by the integral test for convergence.

The test is typically proved in contrapositive form:

- If $\sum_{n=1}^{\infty} a_n$ converges, then $\lim_{n \to \infty} a_n = 0$.

If s_n are the partial sums of the series, then the assumption that the series converges means that

$$\lim_{n \to \infty} s_n = s$$

for some number s. Then

$$\lim_{n \to \infty} a_n = \lim_{n \to \infty} (s_n - s_{n-1}) = s - s = 0.$$

The assumption that the series converges means that it passes Cauchy's convergence test: for every $\varepsilon > 0$ there is a number N such that

$$|a_{n+1} + a_{n+2} + \ldots + a_{n+p}| < \varepsilon$$

holds for all n > N and p ≥ 1. Setting p = 1 recovers the definition of the statement

$$\lim_{n \to \infty} a_n = 0.$$

The simplest version of the term test applies to infinite series of real numbers.

a. Visual Calculus
c. First derivative test
b. Nth term
d. Test for Divergence

30. In mathematics, the _____ is a representation of a function as an infinite sum of terms calculated from the values of its derivatives at a single point. It may be regarded as the limit of the Taylor polynomials. If the series is centered at zero, the series is also called a Maclaurin series.

Chapter 11. INFINITE SEQUENCES AND SERIES

    a. 15 theorem
    c. BIBO stability
    b. BDDC
    d. Taylor series

31. In mathematics, the _____, introduced by German mathematician Georg Cantor in 1883 (but discovered in 1875 by Henry John Stephen Smith), is a set of points lying on a single line segment that has a number of remarkable and deep properties. Through consideration of it, Cantor and others helped lay the foundations of modern general topology. Although Cantor himself defined the set in a general, abstract way, the most common modern construction is the Cantor ternary set, built by removing the middle thirds of a line segment.
    a. BDDC
    c. Planar Lamina
    b. 15 theorem
    d. Cantor set

32. The _____ is a plane fractal first described by Waclaw Sierpinski in 1916. The carpet is a generalization of the Cantor set to two dimensions (another is Cantor dust.) Sierpinski demonstrated that this fractal is a universal curve, in that any possible one-dimensional graph, projected onto the two-dimensional plane, is homeomorphic to a subset of the _____.
    a. Siegel disc
    c. BDDC
    b. Sierpinski carpet
    d. 15 theorem

33. Integration is an important concept in mathematics, specifically in the field of calculus and, more broadly, mathematical analysis. Given a function f of a real variable x and an interval [a, b] of the real line, the _____

$$\int_a^b f(x)\, dx ,$$

is defined informally to be the net signed area of the region in the xy-plane bounded by the graph of f, the x-axis, and the vertical lines x = a and x = b.

The term '_____' may also refer to the notion of antiderivative, a function F whose derivative is the given function f.

    a. Integral test for convergence
    c. Integral
    b. Integrand
    d. Indefinite integral

34. In calculus, the _____ is a formula used to find the derivatives of products of functions. It may be stated thus:

$$(f \cdot g)' = f' \cdot g + f \cdot g'$$

or in the Leibniz notation thus:

$$\frac{d}{dx}(u \cdot v) = u \cdot \frac{dv}{dx} + v \cdot \frac{du}{dx}.$$

Discovery of this rule is credited to Gottfried Leibniz, who demonstrated it using differentials. Here is Leibniz's argument: Let u and v be two differentiable functions of x.

a. Quotient Rule
b. Reciprocal Rule
c. Constant factor rule in differentiation
d. Product Rule

35. The _____ are a pair of first order, non-linear, differential equations frequently used to describe the dynamics of biological systems in which two species interact, one a predator and one its prey. They were proposed independently by Alfred J. Lotka in 1925 and Vito Volterra in 1926.

where

- y is the number of some predator;
- x is the number of its prey;
- dy/dt and dx/dt represents the growth of the two populations against time;
- t represents the time; and
- >α, >β, >γ and >δ are parameters representing the interaction of the two species.

When multiplied out, the equations take a form useful for physical interpretation. Their origin should be considered from a more general framework,

where both functions represent per capita growth rates of the prey and predator, respectively.

a. BDDC
b. BIBO stability
c. 15 theorem
d. Lotka-Volterra equations

36. In calculus, the _____ is a shorthand method of finding the derivative of a function that is the reciprocal of a differentiable function, without using the quotient rule or chain rule.

The _____ states that the derivative of 1 / g(x) is given by

$$\frac{d}{dx}\left(\frac{1}{g(x)}\right) = \frac{-g'(x)}{(g(x))^2}$$

where $g(x) \neq 0$.

The _____ is derived from the quotient rule, with the numerator f(x) = 1. Then,

It is also possible to derive the _____ from the chain rule, by a process very much like that of the derivation of the quotient rule.

a. Differentiation rules
b. Quotient Rule
c. Constant factor rule in differentiation
d. Reciprocal Rule

37. In mathematics, an _____ is an infinite series of the form

$$\sum_{n=0}^{\infty}(-1)^n a_n,$$

with $a_n \geq 0$ (or $a_n \leq 0$) for all n. A finite sum of this kind is an alternating sum. An _____ converges if the terms a_n converge to 0 monotonically.

a. Uniform convergence
b. Extreme value
c. Alternating Series
d. Infinite series

38. The _____ converges:

$$\sum_{k=1}^{\infty}\frac{(-1)^{k+1}}{k} = 1 - \frac{1}{2} + \frac{1}{3} - \frac{1}{4} + \cdots = \ln 2 = 0.693\,147\,180\ldots.$$

This equality is a consequence of the Mercator series, the Taylor series for the natural logarithm. Another equality, similar in form to Mercator's series, is:

$$\sum_{k=0}^{\infty}\frac{(-1)^k}{2k+1} = 1 - \frac{1}{3} + \frac{1}{5} - \frac{1}{7} + \cdots = \arctan(1) = \frac{\pi}{4}.$$

This is a consequence of the Taylor series representation of the inverse tangent function (which has a radius of convergence of 1.)

The nth partial sum of the diverging harmonic series,

$$H_n = \sum_{k=1}^{n}\frac{1}{k},$$

is called the nth harmonic number.

a. AUSM
b. ACTRAN
c. Alternating harmonic series
d. ALGOR

39. In mathematics, a series or integral is said to be _____ if it converges, but it does not converge absolutely.

More precisely, a series $\sum_{n=0}^{\infty} a_n$ is said to converge conditionally if $\lim_{m \to \infty} \sum_{n=0}^{m} a_n$ exists and is a finite number (not ∞ or -∞), but $\sum_{n=0}^{\infty} |a_n| = \infty$.

A classical example is given by

$$1 - \frac{1}{2} + \frac{1}{3} - \frac{1}{4} + \frac{1}{5} - \cdots = \sum_{n=1}^{\infty} \frac{(-1)^{n+1}}{n}$$

which converges to ln 2 , but is not absolutely convergent

The simplest examples of _____ series (including the one above) are the alternating series.

a. Telescoping series
b. Conditionally convergent
c. Converge absolutely
d. Geometric series

40. In mathematics, a series (or sometimes also an integral) is said to _____ if the sum (or integral) of the absolute value of the summand or integrand is finite.

More precisely, a real or complex-valued series $\sum_{n=0}^{\infty} a_n$ is said to _____ if $\sum_{n=0}^{\infty} |a_n| < \infty$.

Absolute convergence is vitally important to the study of infinite series because on the one hand, it is strong enough that such series retain certain basic properties of finite sums -- the most important ones being rearrangement of the terms and convergence of products of two infinite series -- that are unfortunately not possessed by all convergent series. On the other hand absolute convergence is weak enough to occur very often in practice.

a. Sequence transformation
b. Geometric series
c. Telescoping series
d. Converge absolutely

41. In mathematics, the _____ is a criterion for the convergence (a convergence test) of an infinite series

$$\sum_{n=1}^{\infty} a_n.$$

Chapter 11. INFINITE SEQUENCES AND SERIES

It is particularly useful in connection with power series.

The _____ was developed first by Cauchy and so is sometimes known as the Cauchy _____ or Cauchy's radical test.
The _____ uses the number

$$C = \limsup_{n \to \infty} \sqrt[n]{|a_n|},$$

where 'lim sup' denotes the limit superior, possibly ∞.

a. Dirichlet integral
b. Binomial series
c. Root Test
d. Related rates

42. This article will state and prove the _____ for differentiation, and then use it to prove these two formulas.

The _____ for differentiation states that for every natural number n, the derivative of $f(x) = x^n$ is $f'(x) = nx^{n-1}$, that is,

$$(x^n)' = nx^{n-1}.$$

The _____ for integration

$$\int x^n \, dx = \frac{x^{n+1}}{n+1} + C$$

for natural n is then an easy consequence. One just needs to take the derivative of this equality and use the _____ and linearity of differentiation on the right-hand side.

a. Power Rule
b. Dirichlet integral
c. Limits of integration
d. Hyperbolic angle

43. In mathematics, the _____ is a way to approximately calculate the definite integral

$$\int_a^b f(x) \, dx.$$

The _____ works by approximating the region under the graph of the function f by a trapezoid and calculating its area. It follows that

$$\int_a^b f(x)\, dx \approx (b-a)\frac{f(a)+f(b)}{2}.$$

To calculate this integral more accurately, one first splits the interval of integration [a,b] into n smaller subintervals, and then applies the _____ on each of them. One obtains the composite _____:

$$\int_a^b f(x)\, dx \approx \frac{b-a}{n}\left[\frac{f(a)+f(b)}{2} + \sum_{k=1}^{n-1} f\left(a + k\frac{b-a}{n}\right)\right].$$

This can alternatively be written as:

$$\int_a^b f(x)\, dx \approx \frac{b-a}{2n}\left(f(x_0) + 2f(x_1) + 2f(x_2) + \cdots + 2f(x_{n-1}) + f(x_n)\right)$$

where

$$x_k = a + k\frac{b-a}{n}, \text{ for } k = 0, 1, \ldots, n$$

(one can also use a non-uniform grid.)

a. 15 theorem
c. BDDC
b. BIBO stability
d. Trapezoidal Rule

44. In mathematics, a _____ is a constant multiplicative factor of a certain object. For example, in the expression $9x^2$, the _____ of x^2 is 9.

The object can be such things as a variable, a vector, a function, etc.

a. Leading coefficient
c. Coefficient
b. Difference polynomial
d. Degree of the polynomial

45. In mathematics, a _____ (in one variable) is an infinite series of the form

$$f(x) = \sum_{n=0}^{\infty} a_n (x-c)^n = a_0 + a_1(x-c)^1 + a_2(x-c)^2 + a_3(x-c)^3 + \cdots$$

Chapter 11. INFINITE SEQUENCES AND SERIES

where a_n represents the coefficient of the nth term, c is a constant, and x varies around c (for this reason one sometimes speaks of the series as being centered at c

In many situations c is equal to zero, for instance when considering a Maclaurin series.

a. Differential calculus
b. Mountain pass theorem
c. Caccioppoli set
d. Power series

46. Trigonometry is a branch of mathematics that deals with triangles, particularly those plane triangles in which one angle has 90 degrees (right triangles.) Trigonometry deals with relationships between the sides and the angles of triangles and with the _____ functions, which describe those relationships.

Trigonometry has applications in both pure mathematics and in applied mathematics, where it is essential in many branches of science and technology.

a. 15 theorem
b. Trigonometric functions
c. Trigonometric integrals
d. Trigonometric

47. In mathematics, a _____ is any series of the form:

$$\frac{1}{2}A_o + \sum_{n=1}^{\infty}(A_n \cos nx + B_n \sin nx).$$

It is called a Fourier series when the terms A_n and B_n have the form:

$$A_n = \frac{1}{\pi}\int_0^{2\pi} f(x)\cos nx\, dx \quad (n = 0, 1, 2, \ldots)$$

$$B_n = \frac{1}{\pi}\int_0^{2\pi} f(x)\sin nx\, dx \quad (n = 1, 2, 3, \ldots)$$

where f is an integrable function.

It is not that case that every _____ is a Fourier Series. A particular question of interest is given a _____, for which values of x does the series converge.

a. Palais-Smale compactness condition
b. P-Laplacian
c. Nash-Moser theorem
d. Trigonometric series

48. In mathematics, _____, first defined by the mathematician Daniel Bernoulli and generalized by Friedrich Bessel, are canonical solutions y(x) of Bessel's differential equation:

Chapter 11. INFINITE SEQUENCES AND SERIES

$$x^2\frac{d^2y}{dx^2} + x\frac{dy}{dx} + (x^2 - \alpha^2)y = 0$$

for an arbitrary real or complex number α (the order of the Bessel function.) The most common and important special case is where α is an integer n.

Although α and −α produce the same differential equation, it is conventional to define different _____ for these two orders (e.g., so that the _____ are mostly smooth functions of α.)

    a. 15 theorem
    c. Logarithmic integral function
    b. Multiplication theorem
    d. Bessel functions

49. The _____ is a test to determine if a relation or its graph is a function or not. For a relation or graph to be a function, it can have at most a single y-value for each x-value. Thus, a vertical line drawn at any x-position on the graph of a function will intersect the graph at most once.

    a. BIBO stability
    c. 15 theorem
    b. BDDC
    d. Vertical Line Test

50. In mathematical analysis, the _____ states that for each value between the least upper bound and greatest lower bound of the image of a continuous function there is a corresponding value in its domain mapping to the original. _____

- Version I. The _____ states the following: If the function y = f(x) is continuous on the interval [a, b], and u is a number between f(a) and f(b), then there is a c ∈ [a, b] such that f(c) = u.

- Version II. Suppose that I is an interval [a, b] in the real numbers R and that f : I → R is a continuous function. Then the image set f(I) is also an interval, and either it contains [f(a), f(b)], or it contains [f(b), f(a)]; that is,

    f(I) ⊇ [f(a), f(b)], or f(I) ⊇ [f(b), f(a)].

It is frequently stated in the following equivalent form: Suppose that f : [a, b] → R is continuous and that u is a real number satisfying f(a) < u < f(b) or f(a) > u > f(b.) Then for some c ∈ [a, b], f(c) = u.

This captures an intuitive property of continuous functions: given f continuous on [1, 2], if f(1) = 3 and f(2) = 5 then f must take the value 4 somewhere between 1 and 2.

    a. ACTRAN
    c. Intermediate Value Theorem
    b. AUSM
    d. ALGOR

51. In calculus, the _____ is a method of finding the derivative of a function that is the quotient of two other functions for which derivatives exist.

Chapter 11. INFINITE SEQUENCES AND SERIES

If the function one wishes to differentiate, f(x), can be written as

$$f(x) = \frac{g(x)}{h(x)}$$

and h(x) ≠ 0, then the rule states that the derivative of g(x) / h(x) is equal to:

$$\frac{d}{dx}f(x) = f'(x) = \frac{g'(x)h(x) - g(x)h'(x)}{[h(x)]^2}.$$

Or, more precisely, if all x in some open set containing the number a satisfy h(x) ≠ 0; and g'(a) and h'(a) both exist; then, f'(a) exists as well and:

$$f'(a) = \frac{g'(a)h(a) - g(a)h'(a)}{[h(a)]^2}.$$

The derivative of (4x − 2) / (x² + 1) is:

$$\frac{d}{dx}\left[\frac{(4x-2)}{x^2+1}\right] = \frac{(x^2+1)(4) - (4x-2)(2x)}{(x^2+1)^2}$$
$$= \frac{(4x^2+4) - (8x^2-4x)}{(x^2+1)^2} \qquad = \frac{-4x^2+4x+4}{(x^2+1)^2}$$

In the example above, the choices

g(x) = 4x − 2
h(x) = x² + 1

were made. Analogously, the derivative of sin(x) / x² (when x ≠ 0) is:

$$\frac{\cos(x)x^2 - \sin(x)2x}{x^4}$$

Another example is:

$$f(x) = \frac{2x^2}{x^3}$$

whereas g(x) = 2x² and h(x) = x³, and g'(x) = 4x and h'(x) = 3x².

    a. Reciprocal Rule
    c. Quotient Rule
    b. Differentiation rules
    d. Product rule

52. In mathematics, the _____ of a power series is a non-negative quantity, either a real number or ∞, that represents a domain (within the radius) in which the series will converge. Within the _____, a power series converges absolutely and uniformly on compacta as well. If the series converges, it is the Taylor series of the analytic function to which it converges inside its _____.

    a. Principal values
    c. Motor variable
    b. Radius of convergence
    d. Movable singularity

53. In calculus, _____ gives a sequence of approximations of a differentiable function around a given point by polynomials (the Taylor polynomials of that function) whose coefficients depend only on the derivatives of the function at that point. The theorem also gives precise estimates on the size of the error in the approximation. The theorem is named after the mathematician Brook Taylor, who stated it in 1712, though the result was first discovered 41 years earlier in 1671 by James Gregory.

    a. Leibniz differential
    c. Continuous function
    b. Taylor's theorem
    d. Complex analysis

54. In the mathematical field of numerical analysis, a _____ is a parametric curve important in computer graphics and related fields. Generalizations of Bezier curves to higher dimensions are called Bezier surfaces, of which the Bezier triangle is a special case.

Bezier curves were widely publicized in 1962 by the French engineer Pierre B>ézier, who used them to design automobile bodies.

    a. 15 theorem
    c. BDDC
    b. BIBO stability
    d. Bezier curve

55. In mathematics, the _____ $\binom{n}{k}$ is the coefficient of the x^k term in the polynomial expansion of the binomial power $(1 + x)^n$.

In combinatorics, $\binom{n}{k}$ is interpreted as the number of k-element subsets (the k-combinations) of an n-element set, that is the number of ways that k things can be 'chosen' from a set of n things. Hence, $\binom{n}{k}$ is often read as 'n choose k' and is called the choose function of n and k.

    a. Constraint counting
    c. BDDC
    b. 15 theorem
    d. Binomial coefficient

56. In mathematics, the _____ generalizes the purely algebraic formula of the binomial theorem to complex values of α. It is also a special case of a Newton series. The _____ is the series

Chapter 11. INFINITE SEQUENCES AND SERIES

$$(1+x)^\alpha = \sum_{k=0}^{\infty} \binom{\alpha}{k} x^k = \sum_{k=0}^{\infty} \frac{\prod_{a=0}^{k-1}(\alpha-a)\, x^k}{k!}$$

where α is a complex number and

$$\binom{\alpha}{k} = \frac{\alpha(\alpha-1)(\alpha-2)\cdots(\alpha-k+1)}{k!}$$

is the (generalized) binomial coefficient (if α is a non negative integer, then the (α + 1) th term and all later terms in the series are zero, since each one contains a factor equal to (α − α): thus, in that case, the summation reduces to the algebraic binomial formula.)

- a. Binomial series
- b. Fundamental Theorem of Calculus
- c. Leibniz formula
- d. Taylor's theorem

57. In mathematics, a (topological) _____ is defined as follows: let I be an interval of real numbers (i.e. a non-empty connected subset of $\mathbb{R}$); then a _____ γ is a continuous mapping $\gamma : I \to X$, where X is a topological space. The _____ γ is said to be simple if it is injective, i.e. if for all x, y in I, we have $\gamma(x) = \gamma(y) \implies x = y$. If I is a closed bounded interval $[a, b]$, we also allow the possibility $\gamma(a) = \gamma(b)$ (this convention makes it possible to talk about closed simple _____.)

- a. Prolate cycloid
- b. Closed curve
- c. Tractrix
- d. Curve

58. The _____, named after the mathematician Ehrenfried Walther von Tschirnhaus, is a plane curve which is defined by either of these formulae:

  $y^2 = x^3 + 3x^2$

  $a = r\cos^3(\theta / 3.)$

- a. Dolbeault operator
- b. Strophoid
- c. Kampyle of Eudoxus
- d. Tschirnhausen cubic

Chapter 1

1. a	2. d	3. b	4. a	5. a	6. d	7. c	8. b	9. d	10. d
11. d	12. d	13. d	14. c	15. c	16. d	17. d	18. d	19. d	20. d
21. d	22. b	23. d	24. d	25. d	26. d	27. c	28. d	29. a	30. a
31. d	32. d	33. c	34. b	35. d	36. d	37. d	38. c	39. d	40. b
41. d	42. d	43. a	44. d	45. a	46. b	47. d	48. d	49. a	50. d
51. d	52. c	53. c	54. d	55. a	56. d	57. b	58. d	59. b	60. d
61. c	62. a	63. d	64. a	65. d	66. b	67. d	68. d	69. b	70. d
71. d	72. b								

Chapter 2

1. d	2. d	3. d	4. d	5. d	6. b	7. a	8. c	9. d	10. b
11. a	12. b	13. b	14. b	15. d	16. d	17. a	18. d	19. d	20. d
21. a	22. d	23. c	24. d	25. d	26. c	27. c	28. b	29. d	30. b
31. a	32. d	33. d	34. c	35. d	36. b	37. d	38. d	39. a	

Chapter 3

1. d	2. d	3. d	4. d	5. c	6. b	7. b	8. d	9. d	10. c
11. a	12. d	13. c	14. d	15. b	16. d	17. d	18. b	19. c	20. a
21. d	22. d	23. d	24. d	25. b	26. d	27. d	28. d	29. c	30. c
31. d	32. d	33. d	34. c	35. c	36. d	37. c	38. a	39. d	40. d
41. d	42. d	43. d	44. c	45. c	46. d	47. a	48. b	49. c	50. d
51. d	52. a	53. d	54. b	55. d	56. b	57. c	58. d	59. d	60. d
61. c	62. c	63. d	64. a	65. b	66. a	67. b	68. d	69. d	70. a
71. a	72. a	73. d	74. d	75. d	76. d	77. c	78. d	79. d	

Chapter 4

1. d	2. d	3. d	4. d	5. d	6. d	7. d	8. d	9. a	10. a
11. a	12. d	13. d	14. c	15. a	16. b	17. d	18. d	19. d	20. b
21. b	22. c	23. d	24. b	25. a	26. d	27. d	28. d	29. a	30. b
31. a	32. b	33. d	34. c	35. c	36. d	37. b	38. b	39. a	40. c
41. d	42. d	43. d	44. c	45. d	46. b				

Chapter 5

1. c	2. d	3. d	4. d	5. b	6. d	7. c	8. c	9. d	10. d
11. d	12. d	13. c	14. d	15. b	16. d	17. a	18. d	19. a	20. b
21. a	22. d								

Chapter 6

1. c	2. d	3. c	4. d	5. c	6. c	7. d	8. d	9. a	10. d
11. d	12. d	13. c	14. d	15. c	16. a	17. d	18. d	19. b	20. a
21. a	22. d	23. d	24. b	25. d	26. c	27. a	28. b	29. d	

ANSWER KEY

Chapter 7
1. a	2. d	3. a	4. a	5. d	6. b	7. a	8. b	9. d	10. b
11. d	12. d	13. a	14. b	15. d	16. d	17. d	18. b	19. d	20. d
21. d	22. b	23. d	24. c	25. d	26. b	27. d			

Chapter 8
1. b	2. a	3. d	4. d	5. b	6. d	7. b	8. d	9. d	10. d
11. b	12. c	13. d	14. a	15. d	16. a	17. c	18. d	19. b	20. b
21. d	22. d	23. d	24. a	25. c	26. d	27. c	28. c	29. d	30. b
31. d	32. a	33. c	34. d	35. d					

Chapter 9
1. d	2. d	3. d	4. b	5. b	6. a	7. a	8. b	9. a	10. c
11. b	12. d	13. d	14. d	15. d	16. d	17. a	18. c	19. d	20. c
21. d	22. d	23. d	24. c	25. c	26. d	27. c	28. d	29. d	30. c
31. c	32. c	33. d	34. c	35. d	36. c	37. d			

Chapter 10
1. d	2. a	3. b	4. d	5. d	6. c	7. d	8. d	9. a	10. d
11. c	12. a	13. a	14. d	15. b	16. b	17. b	18. b	19. d	20. b
21. d	22. a	23. a	24. d	25. c	26. a	27. a	28. a	29. a	30. d
31. b	32. a	33. c	34. d	35. d	36. d	37. b	38. d	39. d	40. c
41. b	42. c	43. c	44. a	45. c	46. d	47. d	48. b	49. b	50. a
51. d	52. c								

Chapter 11
1. d	2. d	3. d	4. b	5. d	6. d	7. d	8. c	9. b	10. c
11. b	12. b	13. b	14. b	15. d	16. d	17. d	18. c	19. a	20. a
21. d	22. d	23. c	24. d	25. c	26. d	27. d	28. d	29. d	30. d
31. d	32. b	33. c	34. d	35. d	36. d	37. c	38. c	39. b	40. d
41. c	42. a	43. d	44. c	45. d	46. d	47. d	48. d	49. d	50. c
51. c	52. b	53. b	54. d	55. d	56. a	57. d	58. d		

www.ingramcontent.com/pod-product-compliance
Lightning Source LLC
Chambersburg PA
CBHW082205230426
43672CB00015B/2903